DR. MARTHA
CANNON
of
UTAH

The Unexpected Victorian Life
of America's First Female State Senator

JOAN JACOBSON

THE
History
PRESS

Published by The History Press
Charleston, SC
www.historypress.com

First published 2023

Manufactured in the United States

ISBN 9781467155076

Library of Congress Control Number: 2023938354

Persons attempting to find a motive in this narrative will be prosecuted; persons attempting to find a moral in it will be banished; persons attempting to find a plot in it will be shot. BY ORDER OF THE AUTHOR.

—*Mark Twain,* The Adventures of Huckleberry Finn, *1884*

CONTENTS

Preface

THE VICTORIAN ERA

Kookier Than Corsets and Crochet

I first heard the story of the polygamous wife beating her husband for Utah State Senate during a tour of the Salt Lake City Cemetery. My churchy Lutheran group was playing tourist in Mormon country, gawking at Dr. Cannon's grave. She, her husband and his five other wives were (and still are) all lined up like matches in a matchbook. It was such a great story that it couldn't be true. Our tour guide had to be jonesing for a tip. It had to be a legend or, at a minimum, exaggerated.

An unrepentant fact-checker, I went straight back to my hotel room and started investigating.

It was true. Dozens of yellowed newspaper clippings from 1896, available online with a click, confirmed it—all of it.

Truth really is stranger than fiction.

And more sensational and salacious to boot.

WHY ISN'T SENATOR DR. Martha Hughes Cannon famous? Offhandedly proud is how Utah treats her. A sharp lookout spots mentions in a few places throughout Salt Lake City. Her face is stitched onto a weird quilted banner at the visitor's center. Tour guides may or may not mention her. Her statue stands outside the Utah State Supreme Court chambers, a peculiar placement considering her most significant interaction with the law was absconding abroad to avoid a subpoena.

Most significant, I guess, is the Dr. Martha Hughes Cannon Building, a nondescript twentieth-century office building out by the airport, headquarters for the Utah Department of Health. I spent a morning there annoying Utahns with a pop history quiz. Standing at the entrance underneath the big letters spelling out her name, I asked people coming and going if they knew who Martha Hughes Cannon was. They all answered politely, because that's what Utahns do. A sole self-described "history nerd" who works in the building knew all about Mattie. Other employees had a vague notion she was an "influential woman in Utah history," either a safe bet or they'd seen the plaque inside the building. As for nonemployees, "no clue" was the unanimous response.

To their credit, a few of my clueless quiz-takers asked to learn more about Mattie (the nickname she went by). I was happy to oblige. My favorite response came from the tattooed and bearded hipster guy, born and raised in Utah, who listened attentively and then blurted out, "Wait. What? In *Utah?*"

That's right. Our country's first female state senator was elected in *Utah*.

Maybe Mattie's not famous because a feminist politician doesn't fit our stereotype of the polygamous Mormon wife. She doesn't fit our conception of the hands-on-the-plow pioneer woman either. And a female physician doesn't mesh with our idea of the prim and proper Victorian lady who blushed at the word *legs*.

But what if those stereotypes are wrong?

IN THE 1980s, DURING the heyday of Victorian nostalgia, when cupolaed bed-and-breakfasts were all the rage, I wrote for *Victorian Homes* magazine and guided tours in a nineteenth-century log mansion outside Denver. Part of my schtick was relating that the mansion's original owner, Dr. Josepha Douglas, was a woman physician. My tourists were surprised to learn about a woman doctor who lived in Colorado one hundred years earlier. And Dr. Jo wasn't the only one. In 1899, a Black woman, Dr. Justina Ford, established her medical practice in Denver's Five Points neighborhood. She practiced for fifty years.

The story of Dr. Mattie Hughes Cannon in Utah lit a fire under that old kettle of Victorian trivia. An idea bubbled to the surface. Maybe Dr. Mattie's story isn't a historical anomaly at all. Funny as it sounds, maybe her doctor-polygamous wife-politician tale is not a historical aberration. Maybe it's an encapsulation of the entire Victorian world and all its weirdness.

Victorian life was not exactly prim and proper. *Library of Congress, LC-DIG-ppmsca-04666.*

Don't get me wrong. Dr. Cannon's own neighbors and fellow citizens across the United States found this polygamous wife beating her husband at the polls story every bit as hilarious as you. The *Salt Lake Tribune* suggested that Mr. Cannon (Angus was his first name) go home and break a bouquet over her head. The story was the 1896 version of clickbait. It ran in newspapers from Maine to Montana. Monogamous husbands and wives all over the country were snapping the newsprint open over their crocheted tablecloths, exclaiming over their morning coffee, "Honey, you won't believe what those crazy Mormons did now!"

Truth is, though, Mormondom was not that much crazier than the rest of the country. The entire nineteenth century was a little wacky—maybe as crazy as our own twenty-first century. It was certainly as contradictory. This was the prudish era that birthed Sylvester Graham, who invented his eponymous cracker (think s'mores) as a cure for masturbation. It was the century of the "Cult of True Womanhood," which held up the frigid and squeamish female as the "ideal woman." It was also the century that established dozens of "free love" communes, including one where only women were allowed to climax. (You can't make this stuff up.)

Many of our great-great-great-grandparents were so reticent about sex that they coined a dictionary full of delightful euphemisms for the act from "amorous congress" and "bread and butter" to "riding St. George." At the same time, "Walter," the English language's most prolific pornographer, wrote a "memoir" titled *My Secret Life* (four thousand pages and one million words), employing a vocabulary that would make a Netflix comedian blush. For your reading pleasure, get all eleven volumes for ninety-nine cents on Amazon. It was an era that mostly limited women to the professions of maid, teacher and sex worker, but it also educated more women physicians than any time up to the 1970s. Women were allowed to vote in only a handful of western states (including Utah), and yet, a woman ran for president in 1872.

How can we reconcile these contradictions? What were the 1800s really like? Imagine a historian a century from now, looking back on us. Does their research show our era epitomized by internet porn or evangelical purity balls? Our century is going to be every bit the headscratcher for future historians that the nineteenth century is for us: confusing, contradictory and positively peculiar.

So, this book is not just about Dr. Mattie Hughes, also known as Senator Martha Hughes Cannon. It's a deep dive into the weird world that created Mattie, from Wales, where she was born; to Utah, where she grew up; to Michigan, where she went to med school; back to Utah, where she was wed; over to England, where she hid from the law; and then back to Utah, where she practiced medicine and served four years in the state senate.

Her world—its economy, hardships, opportunities, religion, science, attitudes and culture—shaped her and led directly, by fits and starts, to our modern situation. Yet here in the early twenty-first century, we can't figure out what to make of it. When you're done with this book, you still won't get it, but you'll have been entertained, informed, surprised and maybe even shocked. Revel in the weirdness. Feel free to laugh. Just know that while Dr. Mattie's world was decidedly weird, it was no weirder than our own. A century or more in the future, people are going to be laughing and shaking their heads over our era. And that's OK.

WRAP YOUR HEAD AROUND this: the second Mormon prophet Brigham Young's Utah was an aggressively progressive place, at least as far as (white) women were concerned. Never mind that today's Church of Jesus Christ of Latter-day Saints is a profoundly conservative crowd. In the Victorian era, Mormonism was brand-new and radical. Sure, the whole polygamy thing harkened back three thousand years to Old Testament patriarchs. Still, much of what they did was forward-thinking. Sending missionaries from Utah

FEMALE SUFFRAGE.
Wouldn't it put just a little too much power into the hands of Brigham Young, and his tribe?

Mormons supported female suffrage. Gentiles? Not so much. *Library of Congress, LC-USZC2-787.*

across the ocean to the Old World to promote a uniquely American religion was not a conservative thing to do. Neither was building and peopling a spanking-new Kingdom of God in the middle of the godforsaken desert of Utah. Brigham Young couldn't accomplish either of these things, much less both, by repressing over half the believers—women.

Victorian Mormons were proud to lead the way in empowering women. "Verily the world progresseth," exclaimed the *Deseret Evening News* on March 17, 1869, celebrating a congressional bill to give Utah women the right to vote. Edited by Mattie Hughes Cannon's future brother-in-law, George Q. Cannon, the newspaper gushed on, "The plan of giving our ladies the right of suffrage is, in our opinion, a most excellent one."

"Hurrah for Utah!" exclaimed Susan B. Anthony. *Library of Congress, LC-USZ61-791.*

The Mormon writer was being disingenuous, seeing as how the bill he touted was titled "A Bill to Discourage Polygamy in Utah." Congress's idea was that women would vote out polygamy. Still, mixed with the snark, he enthused a sincerely progressive attitude: "[I]f the wish is to try the experiment of giving females the right to vote in the Republic, we know of no place where the experiment can be so safely tried as in this Territory. Our ladies can prove to the world that in a society where men are worthy of the name, women can be enfranchised without running wild or becoming unsexed."

Another congressional attempt to punish polygamy, the Cullom Bill, backfired spectacularly. It eventually died in the senate, but not before five thousand Utah ladies gathered in the Old Tabernacle (which wasn't old then, of course) for an "Indignation Meeting" on January 13, 1870. The only men allowed inside were newspaper reporters. The *New York Herald* reported, "It will not be denied that the Mormon women have both brains and tongues." A month later, the Utah Territorial Legislature gave women the right to vote.

Wyoming was the first territory to enfranchise women, but Utah women actually beat Wyoming women to the polls. The first female-cast ballot was dropped into the box from the hand of Brigham Young's own niece Seraph Young in a municipal election in February 1870. It would be another half century before the rest of the country caught up.

So, there was good reason the most famous pioneer for women's rights, Susan B. Anthony, exclaimed, "Hurrah for Utah!" In 1871, Susan B. Anthony and Elizabeth Cady Stanton traveled to Utah at the invitation of Brigham Young and gave a five-hour speech to three hundred women in the tabernacle in Temple Square. Anthony returned to the tabernacle in 1895, the second time with an audience of thousands.

Utah women never voted to end polygamy and lost their right to vote in 1887. But they gained it back in 1896, just in time to vote for our hero, Dr. Martha Hughes Cannon, for Utah State Senate.

ACKNOWLEDGEMENTS

My special thanks go to Don Rosenberry, the Belmar Critique Group, Deb Elstad, Carolyn Reed, Brigette Weier, Paula Stacey and, most significantly, the Utah State Historical Society and J. Willard Marriott Library of the University of Utah.

1

THE POOR AND PUTRID
VICTORIAN WORLD

It's Just Plain Gross

The first woman senator elected in the United States was elected in 1896. In Utah.

She was a physician.

And a polygamous wife.

Number four of six.

She ran against—wait for it—her husband.

She beat him by four thousand votes.

Her name was Dr. Martha Hughes Cannon, and this is the story of her unlikely Victorian life.

As we traipse back in time to her birthplace, Queen Victoria's kingdom (shouldn't that be queendom?), be forewarned.

It stinks.

Literally.

And figuratively, too.

If you imagine the Victorian world as a romantic place of flickering gas lamps, swishy dresses and gleaming top hats, it's time for a smell check. The Victorian world stank, especially in Great Britain, where Mattie (Martha's nickname) was born. Although her parents left for Utah when she was a toddler, she returned to England as a young woman. Her letters home help explain why her family and so many others took off for the United States.

Mattie complained that London was draped in a smelly and "dense yellow fog." Want to see pictures? Go to an exhibit of Claude Monet's fog paintings, or just Google Monet. He painted London's Parliament with the Thames fuzzed out, illuminated by gorgeous splashes of nebulous yellow. That's the poisonous gas sulphur dioxide. It came from burning soft coal. The air smelled like a just-struck match. It was not a momentary sniff, like when you actually strike a match. The city reeked of it for days. The worst days were called "pea soupers." People died.

Then there were the cigars. "They are all smoking, the air is stenched," Mattie wrote.

Topping off that were the odors of sickness. Mattie, a trained physician, recognized the foul aroma of syphilis and the mushroom-like stench of gonorrhea emanating from her English neighbors. She was repulsed. Who wouldn't be?

Is it any wonder her parents had fled to the clean air and moral rectitude of Utah?

Let's get down and dirty. Really dirty. There can be no escaping the Victorian era's putrid glory, even in Utah.

Middle-class Victorians didn't post pictures of bathroom remodels on Facebook. They were lucky to have an outhouse. The poorest folks did their business in a bucket and threw it in the gutter. A fine lady didn't flounce out to the outhouse in a ballgown, nor did she tiptoe through the dark in her nightdress. That's what chamber pots were for—and chambermaids. Wealthy people (or job creators, shall we say) paid servants to dump out their pots and rinse them clean. (You thought chambermaids just opened the windows and changed the sheets?) For poor women, tipping her ladyship's "night soil" into the pit was considered a good job (although probably not by the women who actually did it).

Moving on. Horse manure—lots of it—littered the streets everywhere, even in Salt Lake City. (Some things can't be fixed with religion.) Cities employed people to scoop shit off the streets like snowplow drivers clear the roads today.

Grossed out yet?

Let's take a moment to give thanks for antibiotics, sewage disposal, the EPA and—dare we say it—auto manufacturers.

Cities carted off loads of manure daily. *Public domain.*

NOT DONE. SORRY. FUTURE chapters will be nicer. For the time being, we have personal hygiene to attend to—or not.

There were no antiperspirants in great-great-great-grandma's and great-great-great-grandpa's day, just lots of perfume. Women were discouraged from bathing, as it could lead to sexual thoughts. (Not kidding.) The Mormons were a bit more fastidious on the matter of bathing. Scandinavian converts to Mormonism were advised: "The first step in this important reformation is to wash the whole body at least once a week."

That advice didn't necessarily include a person's hair. Know those fancy up-dos you see in pictures of Victorian ladies? Want to know how they accomplished those? By not washing their hair. Instead, ladies brushed and brushed and brushed and brushed. One hundred strokes every evening pulled out coal soot and miscellaneous grime. Brushing also distributed natural oils from the scalp to the ends. Who needs conditioner?

Now, those one hundred strokes left a lot of hair on the brush. Did our Victorian ladies throw that out? Heavens, no! They tucked their gobs of greasy strands into a pretty "hair receiver" made of bronze, ceramic or crystal. When it came time to get all fancied up for the ball, they stuffed the old hairs back under their hairs that were still attached. Ta-da! Fantastic poufs.

Rest assured that our Mattie Hughes would have none of that. She cut her hair short. Fashion be damned.

On top of her corset, a lady layered thirty-seven pounds of clothing. *Library of Congress, LC-USZ61-791.*

Speaking of fashion, a proper lady wore about thirty-seven pounds of clothing. That's right—pounds. Thirty-seven. (Slackers might get by with just twenty-three pounds.) The poundage began with a chemise, like a light slip. Next came stockings. Her thighs would be clothed in crotchless "pantalets." No panties. Remember that. Over the chemise, the Victorian lady cinched a corset, which scrunched her belly flat and pushed up her breasts. Bras had not yet been invented. Unless she wanted to be a total frump, the lady pulled that corset as tight as she could. If she had a maid or mother to yank it tighter yet, all the better. Ideally, she would wrench her waist down to twenty-two to twenty-three inches.

Here again, we must stop to praise nineteenth-century Mormons. In the land of Utah, where men sought multiple wives, standards could be a little lower. A devout Mormon man, desiring an exalted afterlife thanks to embracing the Principle (that is, polygamy), may well settle for a wife or two or three with a waist as big as, say, twenty-four inches—or maybe even larger. Don't think that wasn't a temptation for a lot of women. Women who enjoyed breathing, for example.

A wire crinoline or bustle separated our Victorian lady's undergarments from her outer pounds of skirts and blouses and jackets and lots and lots of ruffles, pleats and bows. Finally, she buttoned up her boots. And the boots pinched her feet when she walked.

The ridiculousness of all this did not escape the attention of our own Dr. Mattie. In 1897, Senator Dr. Martha Hughes Cannon attended a graduation for the Utah School for the Deaf. A student speaker ridiculed the fashions of the day. Pointedly, she complained that women's boots were "so tight they cannot walk in the paths of righteousness."

FEELING SMUG AND COMFY, walking the paths of righteousness in your one-pound ensemble of a T-shirt, yoga pants and mesh sneakers? Now, let us investigate the very unrighteous Victorian economy. It will weigh on you more heavily than thirty-seven pounds of petticoats and gross you out more than the thought of sliding a chamber pot full of pee and poop under your bed at night.

The kind of stuff you see in the first seasons of *Downton Abbey*—elegant gowns, nine-course banquets and the kindly treatment of servants—makes fantastic TV. But it's as real as the *Real Housewives of Salt Lake City*. On the city streets and country lanes of the Old World, economies were Dickensian. (Think Oliver Twist and his empty bowl.) Mormon missionary to Liverpool Heber C. Kimball said he saw "the rich attired in the most costly dresses, and

Life was brutal. *iStock.*

the next minute was saluted with the cries of the poor with scarce covering sufficient to screen them from the weather."

In Wales, where Mattie was born, unskilled men could choose between working themselves to death in the ironworks, dying of black lung disease from a coalmine, breaking their backs smashing rock or getting crushed in a copper mine.

Even for skilled artisans, Europe offered no dreams, only nightmares of starvation and sleeping in a gutter with your kids. Working people were just half a step from homelessness and death. Is it any wonder the wide-open spaces and big sky of the American frontier sounded like heaven on Earth?

In the nineteenth century, people of every religious persuasion were saving their pennies and fleeing the Old World by the shipful. The rule of thumb was that one penny bought three miles. It took years to save up. To sweeten the temptation to keep going all the way to Utah rather than stop in, say, Minnesota, the Brigham Young Perpetual Emigrating Fund offered loans.

The Hughes family were among tens of thousands who converted. Mom and Dad Hughes packed up little Mattie and her sister and fled the dirty and depressing life of Wales. The family boarded a ship, crossed an ocean and then trekked over a thousand miles.

On foot.

POLYGAMY WAS COMMON IN Utah by the time toddler Mattie Hughes and her family set sail from Liverpool in 1860. Two years earlier, in 1858, when the Hughes family was still saving their pennies back in Wales, Mattie's future husband, Angus Cannon, married his first two wives, sisters Amanda and Sarah Mousley, in one fell swoop.

As you might imagine, polygamy set Victorian tongues a-wagging. People were scandalized! Horrified! Shocked! Even so, families in Great Britain went right on saving their pennies. Why? Why would Mattie's mother and father take her and her sister Mary, at tremendous sacrifice, to a place where their daughters would quite likely, eventually, share their husbands with other wives?

Because for poor and working-class women in the newly industrialized world, there were a lot of things far, far worse than sharing a husband.

The Industrial Revolution wreaked havoc on the value of women's skills. In the prior century, women's traditional skills, such as baking, brewing, cheese making, spinning and weaving, were valued by families and neighbors. Once machines took over, very few good-paying jobs were left for women. They could be clerks, seamstresses and laundresses. None of those jobs paid for both a bed *and* food. A single working woman had to choose one or the other. If she couldn't make up her mind, she would go to the workhouse or find supplementary income. At the workhouse, she'd get both a lousy bed (that means literally crawling with lice) and ghastly food but at a huge cost. The idea behind the workhouse was that humiliation, disease, malnutrition and grueling work would terrify women so much that they'd do anything to avoid it.

And they did. Supplementary income was easy to find. Remember the "no panties" thing? When a single woman didn't want to choose between a bed and food, she could lift her skirts in an alley for a gentleman. See? When you pretty much know for certain that, eventually, poverty will drive you to prostitution, polygamy doesn't seem so shocking.

Why not just get married monogamously? That's what you're thinking, and that was the simple answer in the 1800s, too, but the law of supply and demand made that easier said than done. Thanks to wars, mine cave-ins and industrial accidents, nineteenth-century demographics were way out of whack. Women outnumbered men by a distressing degree. This was the Victorian blight of "surplus women," which is what they called it. Really. Surplus women were a problem everywhere, except in the American West.

Downton Abbey watchers are probably thinking, "A woman could become a servant! Servants got a cute uniform, bed, food and such a nice, big house to work in!" OK, OK. Servant jobs were an option, but real servanthood was no *Downton Abbey*–style employment overseen by the kindly Seventh Earl of Grantham and his honorable heir-presumptive Matthew Crawley. Real-life servants worked six and a half days a week from before sunrise to deep into the night. They got Sunday mornings off to walk to church, sit in church and walk back from church, plus a half day a month for personal business.

Still, that's better than sleeping on the street and starving. Right?

Maybe.

Masters promised that servanthood prepared a girl for married life. That was a pretty good recruitment ploy. It was, however—how to say this in a demure Victorian manner—bunkum and twaddle. Women servants were not allowed to date or marry, but they were "fair game" for the men of the esteemed family. Many a servant girl was raped, and others were seduced. The lords of the manor didn't have any reason to make a distinction between the two. When a master impregnated his servant, the law protected the man 100 percent. England's 1834 Poor Law banned child support. Meanwhile, it was the servant girl's "undoing" forever. She was dismissed "without reference" and barred from ever getting another servant job. Not to mention that she was unmarriageable to boot. So, back to choosing between a bed and food, going to the workhouse or lifting her skirts for supplementary income—but now with a baby in tow.

So, all things considered, the wide-open spaces of Utah, where every woman was *guaranteed* a husband, looked pretty good. Nineteenth-century Mormondom was a land of pious polygamists eager to scoop up old maids, widows and even divorcées. Forget choosing between a bed and food; every woman could have her own house with a bedroom, garden and a couple chickens. She could have a private outhouse and no one else's poop to tote!

No reason to stop saving those pennies. Get on a boat. Lace up those pinchy walking boots. Time to walk one thousand miles on the path toward righteousness. Zion awaits.

BEFORE WE SET OFF for Utah with Mattie's family, let's take a detour into Victorian sex—or lack of it.

2
CRAZY CULT

True Woman and Piano Pants

Any Victorian house tour guide worth their salt tells the story of the prudes who dressed their pianos' legs in frilly pantalettes so as not to arouse the passions of their husbands, sons and male guests. It's guaranteed to get the group giggling.

Serious historians say the joke's on us. Pantalooned piano legs were not a thing—at least not any more than Pinterest's crocheted condoms. The difference is that we twenty-first-century sophisticates know the Pinterest post is a gag. Our maybe-a-little-more-gullible Victorian ancestors fell for the piano pants story. Two Brits, the marvelously named writers Fanny Trollope and Captain Frederick Marryat, took great delight in spreading their piano pants story. It certainly made Americans look ridiculous, not that we didn't deserve it. Plenty of us bought the story.

The pants for pianos joke has legs (or, shall we say, "limbs") because the era has a reputation for prudery. That's thanks to the "Cult of True Womanhood," which was a real thing. This was the widely circulated idea that women (that is, "virtuous" middle-class and upper-class white women) experience no sexual desire. In 1844, French physician Adam Raciboorski (another fantastic name) averred that "three-fourths of women merely endure the approaches of men."

No problem! Passionlessness was a good thing! Lack of sexual desire was a "civilizing force." Passion impeded progress! Amoral and immoral males could be reined in by the strength of women's virtue. A True Woman would make a finer, more wonderful world, just by keeping her knees together.

Fanny joked that Americans put pants on piano legs. *Public domain, Wikimedia.*

The polygamous Mormons saw it differently. Mormon theology promised exaltation in heaven for men who fathered lots of children with multiple wives. Male passion was exactly the thing needed to populate Zion. So, the Mormon version of True Womanhood said that women were naturally virtuous but welcomed male passion because they wanted babies.

Poppycock, scoffed our Dr. Mattie Hughes Cannon, never one to go with the flow. Often, she wrote to her husband, in no uncertain terms, women actually wished the sexual act would result in a "miss" rather than a "hit."

So, where did the Cult of True Womanhood come from? If you assume it was a continuation of prior centuries of sexual purity and moral propriety, you'd be wrong.

26

PREMARITAL PREGNANCY RATES IN colonial America and the early United States were about the same as they are now (that is, in the 2020s). In the 1700s, 30 percent of births were to unmarried or just-married women. Not much effort was put into policing what teenagers did in the back of the buggy, so to speak. The difference between then and now was that couples were expected to get married before or just after the birth. A pregnant bride was no big deal, but an unmarried mother was a burden on the community. Even so, in the colonial era, a single mother whose lover couldn't or wouldn't marry her was able to fix the predicament by marrying another man; she wasn't "ruined" forever, like her Victorian granddaughter would be.

From the medieval period through the colonial era, women were considered every bit as libidinous as men, lascivious even. Puritan wives whipped off their skirts and jumped into bed as enthusiastic proof of their pious rejection of the Roman Catholic condemnation of sexual desire. Wives had few legal grounds for divorce, but impotence was one. Legs were called legs, and nobody blushed.

What changed?

Industrialization scared the gee willikers out of people.

Religious fervor soothed anxieties.

Chastity bestowed new power upon women, which, ironically enough, led to feminism.

In the meantime, the Cult of True Womanhood was a bucket of cold water thrown on the libidos of Victorian women.

SMOKE-BELCHING FACTORIES ALTERED THE Victorian era's landscape, the minds of people and social structures, all at the same time. Getting ahead no longer required birthing a lot of little farmhands to gather eggs and milk cows. Victorians didn't have a problem sending an eight-year-old boy into a coal mine or a seven-year-old girl into a textile mill, but those were survival jobs for the poor. A go-getter who left the farm to make his fortune in the city didn't need more mouths to feed.

If they wouldn't (or couldn't) keep their hands off each other, Victorian couples actually had a lot of options for contraception, but none worked very well: coitus interruptus, sheep gut condoms ("French letters"), douches, "contraceptive wads" for the vagina, diaphragms ("the wife's protector") and syringes of alum or sulphates of zinc or iron. On the frontier, women drank gunpowder or ate chicken gizzards. You can't make this stuff up.

When the wife's protector failed to protect or the sheep gut broke, respectable married women of the 1800s had little trouble finding an abortion provider. Abortions were legal for most of the century and were a common, albeit dangerous, answer to the problem of "missing your period." There were many methodologies, but the grossest, probably, was affixing leeches to the cervix.

Poor women and the leech averse could go the DIY route, stabbing themselves with knitting needles or swigging a tonic of ergot of rye, slippery elm or "Madame Frain's Famous Female Mixture. The most powerful and effective on earth. For the most obstinate cases. Will not injure the most delicate."

However, "just say no" was the birth control method most enthusiastically promoted. Women were appointed the role of the "no-sayers." You think it would have been a tough sell, but Victorians were geniuses at effective promotions. They *invented* advertising, after all. Rather than tell women they *should* say no, doctors and advice columnists convinced women that they *wanted* to say no. Sex was not just icky, it was old-fashioned! Colonial grandma's wedding with a baby bump was seen as both fogyish and scandalous. *Grandma, how could you?*

Frigidity was all the vogue. A woman of refined taste submitted to the passions of her husband only as often as necessary to provide the correct number of children. Together with abortions and iffy contraception, it worked. Birth rates plummeted, especially among the white, urban, native-born middle class. Premarital pregnancy rates fell. Marital fertility fell from seven-plus children per couple in 1800 to fewer than four in 1900.

Dr. Mattie Hughes (Mrs. Cannon) knew the passionless female was—how to say this with Victorian delicacy—not supported by her personal experience or the scientific study of female physiology.

"Spermatic economy" was a nifty Victorian "scientific" theory. It held that a man's physical energy was linked to his sperm, and every ejaculation dissipated his "life force." If you're going to do it, make it count! "Wasting sperm" drained not only a man's life force but also his ability to accumulate capital. If left unchecked, wasting sperm could lead to unemployment, stock market collapse and economic depression.

Sylvester Graham to the rescue! He invented the Graham cracker to cure masturbation. But rather than leading to the accumulation of capital, it led to s'mores. Campers remain forever grateful.

Alas, Sylvester Graham's crackers did not cure masturbation. *Library of Congress, LC-USZ62-123830.*

But that's not all. The theory of spermatic economy also held that too many ejaculations could beget a man weak, ugly and "idiot" offspring.

With this, we circle right back to the Mormons. Anti-Mormon believers in spermatic economy described the children in Utah as ugly, dirty, weak and stupid. But Richard Burton (the nineteenth-century anthropologist, not the twentieth-century actor), who actually visited Salt Lake City and checked it out, found hordes of children he described as clean, hardy and good-looking. Whatever a person may think about Mormon theology, the polygamists had enough economic vitality to build and populate a new city in the middle of a desolate wilderness. In fifty years, they grew the city from a population of 6,100 to a population of 131,000, erected a temple, founded a university and eventually gifted us with Donny and Marie. Weak and ugly, pshaw.

MANY HISTORIANS BELIEVE THE Victorians weren't the prudes we are told they were and weren't even the prudes they told themselves they were. Victorian sexual behavior was probably not all that different from our own (borax and leeches notwithstanding). What is incontrovertibly different is how they spoke about it (almost never and, when they did, via euphemism, except in porn) and what they wrote about it in the advice columns.

But the evidence is mixed and a little disturbing. Lutheran pastor Sylvanus Stall felt compelled to give this advice to bridegrooms: "Practice in lawful wedlock the arts of the seducer rather than the violence of the man who commits rape....This bud of passion cannot be rudely forced open."

Unfortunately, some young men, reportedly, couldn't force open the bud of passion if they tried, as they were not able to find it. One doctor reported the case of a clueless bridegroom, who, after several nights of frustration, somehow discovered that "the male organ should be introduced into the 'water passage' of the female. The gentleman essayed the experiment on several different occasions without success, and was then compelled to the ludicrous necessity of searching for the place with a candle." A candle! The obvious fire hazard notwithstanding, this persistent dude could not, by any means, be considered a rapist.

Couples could also be cutely loving, especially those who had progressed beyond searching for the hoo hoo with a candle. Civil War–era Judge Joseph Lyman wrote to his wife, Laura, "I anticipate unspeakable delight in your embrace." She wrote back, "How I long to see you....I'll drain your coffers dry next Saturday, I assure you."

Better even than cute was pious. It could have been an altar candle that inspired our determined young dude. In *Right Marital Living*, Ida Craddock wrote, "The nude embrace comes to be respected more and more...when husband and wife shall melt into one another's genital embrace, so that the twain shall be one flesh, and then, as of old, God will walk with the twain the garden of bliss, 'in the cool of the day,' when the heat of ill-regulated passion is no more."

Ah, the scourge of "ill-regulated passion." That was the splash of ice water thrown on the heat of "genital embrace." The Cult of True Womanhood did allow wives, for the first time in western history, to say no to their husbands—but not legally. That had to wait until 1975, when Nebraska became the first state to outlaw marital rape. The True Woman's status of being more moral and highly evolved meant that she could, with the permission of polite society, if not the courts, turn away from an amoral brute.

One can't finish up with the Cult of True Womanhood without noting the coolest unintended consequence of all time: feminism. It stands to reason that if women are intrinsically moral and more highly evolved than men, shouldn't women also lead? Why let those amoral lesser-evolved creatures make all the decisions?

Antifeminists pushed back that women are "too good" for politics, arguing for "separate spheres": home and hearth for exalted and moral women, and economics and politics for dirty and amoral men. Not so fast, argued the moral women of America. The answer to the ills of society, they pleaded in their pretty but very loud way, lay in the vote for women.

Western states pioneered suffrage for women. In the 1890s, Dr. Martha Hughes Cannon and others got elected to the state legislatures in Utah and Colorado. Finally, after a lot of marching, all women in the United States got the right to vote and hold office in 1920.

It all began with the Cult of True Womanhood—sort of.

3

HOLY MATRIMONY IN THE HAYMOW

Joseph Smith and Secret Polygamy

Into this mess of sexual confusion, befuddled biology and religious enthusiasm steps Joseph Smith, the founder of the Church of Jesus Christ of Latter-day Saints, the Mormon prophet who never made it to Utah.

If you're wanting a history of the boy who dug up some golden plates from under a tree and all that, you're reading the wrong book. Nevertheless, before we move on to the emigration story of Mattie Hughes, the circumstances that sent her to medical school, her polygamous marriage, her Senate race against her husband and her election to the Utah State Senate, we need a little context, an origin story. Joseph Smith provides a juicy one.

IT'S A MISTAKE TO assume Americans were uniformly Christian-believing churchgoers from the days of the black-hatted lacy-collared Puritans up through (pick your date) the 1930s, 1960s, 1990s or whenever. Belief in God has varied relatively little, but active church membership has boomed and busted over and over again in U.S. history.

By the 1700s, a general lackadaisicalness had set in among the American colonies' Congregationalists, Anglicans, Quakers, Presbyterians—you name it. Turgid recitations of theological tedium were boring everybody to tears. Preachers decided to rev things up with some humdinger sermons, the most famous (or infamous, take your pick) being Jonathan Edwards's "Sinners in the Hands of an Angry God." Americans were off to the religious races. The population (white, that is) surged back into Sunday services—80 percent!

And they went not just as "attenders" but also as fervent believers. This was the "New Light" of the First Great Awakening.

Then bust.

By 1780, the New Light had sputtered out. All that denouncing of "depravity" (Calvinists' favorite word) had become depressing. A mere 4 percent of North Carolinians attended church. (This is not counting Black Americans or Native Americans, because, back then, who did?) The churchiest colonies were South Carolina and New Hampshire, tied at a measly 16 percent each. It was time for a Second Great Awakening.

Americans wanted something sexier, and boy did they get it. In the early nineteenth century, revival tents of the Second Great Awakening literally shook from the shouting, groaning, fainting and convulsions of the newly saved. It was theological chaos, fanatical and frenzied. People actually tumbled out of their seats in ecstasy. Aroused by all the alleluias, spiritual ecstasy inspired sexual shenanigans outside the tents, behind the bushes. Nowhere was the excitement hotter than it was in western New York, near Palmyra, nicknamed the "Burnt-Over District" on account of the conflagration of religious passion.

This was where Joseph Smith grew up.

In 1823, young Joseph dug up some golden plates covered with hieroglyphics and translated them into English on regular paper—or so the story goes. The golden plates disappeared, but his ink-on-paper version is *still* a hot-seller, quite remarkable considering that the Book of Mormon (the book, not the musical stage play) is hardly a page-turner. Nevertheless, the not-ready-for-five-stars Book of Mormon inspired a new religion, which has grown from six members in 1830 to sixteen million members today.

INCALCULABLY CHARMING, JOSEPH SMITH could sell a yoke to an ox, it was said. He was also a lothario, a liar and, to a lot of people, a prophet of God. One thing he most definitely was not was a progressive pragmatist like his eventual successor, Brigham Young. Keep these two guys straight, because the polygamy that Joseph Smith practiced evolved into something quite different under Brigham Young. Nevertheless, Smith's original version was terrifically salacious. It's a story that must be told.

Joseph married his first wife, Emma, in 1827. It's unclear exactly when Joseph entered his first "plural marriage." Some think it was as early as 1831 or 1833. We know for certain Emma had been neither consulted nor informed, and Joseph Smith and Fanny Alger weren't "sealed for time and eternity" in a fancy ritual in a temple. Indeed, a reported witness to their

Joseph Smith could sell a yoke to an ox. *Library of Congress, LC-DIG-ppmsca-19968.*

nuptials (or maid of honor, if you will) was a woman who peeked through a crack in the door while they went at it in the haymow of a barn.

We do know when Joseph's first "plural marriage" to Fanny ended—in 1837 when Emma caught Joseph and Fanny in the act. Or maybe it was when Fanny got pregnant and Joseph kicked her out. There are different stories, but none end well for Fanny.

Emma put a stop to all this for a while, but Joe was no quitter. By 1839, Joseph had "married" several other women. How did he manage it? Polygamy seemed as weird then as it does now—probably weirder, considering the Cult of True Womanhood thing going on at the time. It didn't escape notice that Joseph had more passion than piety when it came to female relations. But heavens to Betsy, he was handsome! Joseph Smith had a strong and straight nose; big, dreamy eyes; sensual lips; and a head of hair to die for, thick and black à la Patrick Dempsey.

Joseph certainly knew how to spread the joy, and he had broad tastes for sure. In 1842, he was courting thirty-eight-year-old Eliza Snow and, at the same time, pursuing seventeen-year-old Sarah Ann Whitney. His earliest wives ranged in age from fourteen to fifty-eight, and some of them were married to other men.

That's polyandry—a woman with more than one husband.

This is not fake history. It's documented with names and dates.

Zina Huntington married Henry Jacobs in March 1841. On October 27 that same year, while still married to Henry and pregnant with Henry's child, she married Joseph Smith, too, saying she rejoiced to "live in the newly-revealed order of celestial marriage." Henry was apparently cool with this. Zina continued to live with Henry, and they carried on with their "connubial relationship."

In February 1842, Joseph Smith married Mary Elizabeth Rollins Lightner, who continued living with her legal husband, Adam Lightner, until he died in Utah many years later. Also in 1842, Joseph married Marinda Johnson Hyde while her husband, Orson, was abroad in Jerusalem; she did not divorce Orson until 1870. On November 12, 1843, Joseph married

Augusta Cobb, who was still married to an unconverted husband. Joseph married the already married Jane Law in 1844. He asked for only "half her love." William Law could keep the other half. Zina Huntington's sister Prescindia, who had been married to Norman Buell since 1827, married Joseph Smith on December 11, 1841, but continued to be married to and live with Norman until 1846.

Other high-level church leaders were in on the secret (because these plural marriages were quite secret at first) and also enjoyed polyandrous wives. Lydia Godthwait Bailey was abandoned but not divorced when Joseph Smith officiated her wedding to Newel Knight. After Joseph died, Zina Huntington Jacobs married Brigham Young, even though she was still living with and pregnant by her remarkably understanding husband Henry.

As late as 1857, thirteen years after Joseph Smith was killed and five years after the principle went public, Mrs. Eleanor McLean married church leader Parley P. Pratt. She was still married to Hector McLean. Hector was not nearly as understanding as Henry Jacobs. Hector murdered Parley.

According to the *Atlantic* magazine's 1864 account of Mormondom by Fitz-Hugh Ludlow, polyandry survived the trek to Utah in a platonic form. Brigham Young continued marrying already married women but apparently let them return to their original husbands without physical consummation. Just a few years later, the whole polyandry era was set aside and covered up. In 1869, *Utah Magazine* wrote that men are naturally polygamous and women are naturally monogamous, so that's why polygyny is acceptable polygamy and polyandry is not.

EIGHTY-FOUR WIVES OR TWENTY-SEVEN—HOW many women did Joseph Smith marry? The answer depends on who's counting. Some historians tally it up to eighty-four, others forty-eight, thirty-four or a mere twenty-seven. There's a reason history majors take higher math, although it doesn't seem to have helped much in figuring this out. After, let's say, a dozen, does it really matter? More importantly, why? Second Prophet Brigham Young's grandson Kimball Young wrote the obvious in 1954: "It may well be that the doctrine [of plural marriage] was…a rationalization for Smith's own infidelities." (You think?)

None of Smith's 1831–40 escapades in the haymow, et cetera, were solemnized in ritual or in a Temple. And his proposals weren't all that romantic. In one case, he talked Benjamin Johnson into accepting the principle so he could take Benjamin's sister Almera as his wife. Benjamin kept a journal, in which he noted, "Soon after the Prophet was at my house again, where he occupied my sister Almera's room and bed, and then he asked for my younger sister, Esther." Unfortunately for Joseph, Esther was engaged to be married to someone else and declined his offer for marriage. To his credit, Joseph apparently went on his way without too much fuss about it.

Joseph Smith never publicly acknowledged his reputed revelation of the divine doctrine of plural marriage. He divulged the principle to only his many plural wives, closest church associates and legal wife, Emma (who was not impressed). To everybody else, he lied openly and often.

Keeping a secret as big as polygamy can be very taxing, especially when your legal wife is constantly carping against it. Emma, Joseph complained, was annoying. So, in 1842, after nine years of engaging in polygamy on the sly, Joseph wanted to come clean with his seventeen thousand followers. He also wanted Emma to shut up about it. Having failed to convince her of the divine nature of his proclivities, in spite of almost a decade of trying, the man who could sell a yoke to an ox knew this would be the hardest sell of his life. He decided to send up a trial balloon with plausible deniability. He engaged non-Mormon Udney Hay Jacob to write a theological defense of polygamy. Udney titled it *The Peace Maker*, also known (in that typically voluble Victorian style) as *Doctrines of the Millennium: Being a Treatise on Religion and Jurisprudence or a New System of Religion and Politics*.

It flopped.

Read here in the twenty-first century, the most intriguing thing about *The Peace Maker* is that while history remembers it as a defense of polygamy, that subject comes up, half-heartedly, only near the very end. It's mostly a misogynist diatribe. Udney redefines *fornication* to mean the act of a wife disagreeing with her husband—about anything! (Take that, Emma!):

> *Our ladies have long possessed a power (that is, the power to disagree), which by the very nature of things, the nature of woman and the law of God utterly forbid; it must and does produce misery, vanity, confusion, and sorrow both to them and us. You have placed the husband under the law of the wife as long as the wife lives, and at the same time placed the wife under the law of the husband as long as the husband lives! what an absurdity! what an attempt to an impossibility!! what a confusion!*

What a lot of exclamation points!

All sin, Udney rants on, is caused by being "possessed of the effeminate mind *like Eve*." (The italics are Udney's.) Then he lets his readers in on a secret—but not the one you've been waiting for: "Gentleman, the ladies laugh at your pretended authority. They, many of them, hiss at the idea of your being the lords of the creation."

Well, that's true.

Suffice it to say that this twenty-one-page pamphlet is the most delightful vomit of bilge you may ever have the privilege of reading. (It's on the internet if you're so inclined.)

Eventually, on page 16, Udney gets to the subject of polygamy. One wonders why a man who so despises women would want more than one wife, but—it's biblical! Udney starts by referencing the Bible stories of Jacob and his wives Leah and Rachel before—*wham*—putting it right out there on page 17: "By depriving him of the right of marrying more than one wife, you totally annihilate his power of peaceable government over a woman." If a man can be limited to one wife, why not also limit him to "one dollar, one servant, or one cow." Good question, right?

Comparing women to cows is not the most romantic courtship tactic. Misogyny in general is a poor strategy for attracting multiple wives. After *The Peace Maker* flopped, Joseph Smith privately revealed his own "Revelation on the Patriarchical Order of Matrimony, Or Plurality of Wives," in which

Brigham Young, the pragmatist who transported polygamy to Utah. *Getty Museum.*

he threatened to "destroy" Emma. It didn't go over any better. Even though he "canonized" the principle, he continued to lie about it, which is why, perhaps, Mormon polygamy would never have taken off if Joseph hadn't been murdered in 1844.

The first public acknowledgement of the principle was made in 1852 under the much more pragmatic prophet Brigham Young. The tactful Young showed little taste for threats of destruction and even less regard for the bluster of Udney Hay Jacob. Where Udney argued that a husband can divorce a wife but a wife can never divorce a husband, Brigham Young's Utah had the most lenient divorce laws in the country and Mormon wives filed the vast majority of suits. Where Udney blamed all sin on the "effeminate mind," Utah led the nation in giving the vote to effeminate minds. And what would Joseph and Udney make of our Martha Hughes Cannon, the fourth polygamous wife of church leader Angus Cannon, who not only disagreed with her husband but also ran against him for senate and won?

We get ahead of ourselves.

4

UTTER DESTITUTION
TO HAPPY DELUSIONS

Getting the Hell out of Wales

Wales's economy boomed in the Victorian era. Factories and steamships created an insatiable demand for coal and copper from Wales. Mining was (and is) dirty and dangerous, and while it was better than starving, it was no path to riches. Mormon missionaries had easy pickins in Wales, promising new life in a clean and prosperous frontier community—not to mention eternal exaltation in the hereafter.

Mattie was born to Peter and Elizabeth Hughes in Llandudno in 1857. Nowadays, Llandudno is a resort town, but back in the day, most Llandudno men worked in the copper mines. Peter and Elizabeth had a grander future in mind, and if it meant camping on the ground and navigating the sea of grass that is the American Great Plains to get there, they'd do it—on foot.

By the time Mattie was born, Mormons had been acknowledging and publicly practicing polygamy for five years. Who knows what Mattie's parents were thinking when they converted and started saving their pennies for the voyage across the ocean and the trek across the plains. Maybe they looked at their two little daughters and decided it best to go to a place where the girls would be *guaranteed* to find husbands. Maybe it was heartfelt religious conviction. Maybe it was the lure of Utah's clean air and high wages.

Anthropologist Richard F. Burton, also known as Sir Burton or "Ruffian Dick" (you can't make this stuff up), writing just a few years later in his seminal study of pioneer Mormonism, *The City of the Saints*, appreciated the allure of Utah felt by "the English mechanic and collier, and agricultural

Above: Mattie's birthplace was rough terrain. *Getty Museum.*

Left: Cartoonists ridiculed Mormon polygamy. *Library of Congress, LC-USZ62-68768.*

laborer…who, after a life of ignoble drudgery, of toiling through the year from morning till night, are ever threatened with the workhouse."

Unfortunately, the temptations of Mormon Utah weren't obvious to everyone. The unconverted Hughes relatives were enraged. Not only were Elizabeth and Peter heretics (a way bigger deal then than it is now), but they also made the family the butt of jokes. Mattie's parents stayed resolute and left anyhow. They experienced heartbreaking tragedy on the journey, which we'll get to later, but in the long run, it worked out great.

When Mattie returned to the UK decades later as a college-educated American, she was not impressed. "England is horrid," the grown-up Dr. Mattie reported in 1886. "The mode of living among the lower classes is dreadful. We in Utah live like kings as compared to people here." Like Burton, she could see her poor Welsh relations stood "no chance whatever in this over-populated, stereotyped country."

Mattie's family left in great company. Between 1847 and 1869, more than thirty-two thousand Mormon converts abandoned the United Kingdom for the American frontier. Converts who were too poor or impatient could take out a loan from Brigham Young's Perpetual Emigrating Fund. Once in Utah, the emigrants were required to repay their loan to finance the travels of others. (The fund did not actually turn out to be perpetual. It was outlawed under the 1887 anti-Mormon Edmunds-Tucker Act, having already succeeded spectacularly, funding between twenty and thirty-eight thousand journeys.)

About half of the emigrants from the United Kingdom were artisans and skilled tradesmen, such as carpenters, blacksmiths, shoemakers and stonemasons. The rest were semiskilled laborers, miners and farmers, just the mix of folk who second prophet Brigham Young needed to build the new Zion. Very few came from the top echelon, but few from the gutters either.

Boarding ship was a heady experience the Hughes family found out, a harbinger of their future in the new Zion. Charles Dickens, the scathing chronicler of the era's inhumanity (think Bill Sikes from *Oliver Twist*) and greed (Ebenezer Scrooge from *A Christmas Carol*), effused praise for the Mormons he observed boarding a ship for America: "Now, I have seen emigrant ships before this day in June. And these people are so strikingly different from all other people in like circumstances whom I have ever seen, that I wonder aloud, 'what would a stranger suppose these emigrants to be!'" he wrote in *An Uncommercial Traveler.*

Millions fled Europe on emigrant ships. *Library of Congress, LC-USZ62-60319.*

We can witness Mattie and her mother, father and sister board ship through the eyes of Dickens:

> *Two great gangways made of spars and planks connect* [the ship] *with the wharf; and up and down the gangways, perpetually crowding to and fro and in and out, like ants, are the Emigrants who are going to sail in my Emigrant Ship. Some with cabbages, some with loaves of bread, some with cheese and butter, some with milk and beer, some with boxes, beds, and bundles, some with babies, nearly all with children.... To and fro, up and down, aboard and ashore, swarming here and there and everywhere, my Emigrants!*

How did three-year-old Mattie Hughes handle the mayhem? We don't know exactly, but Dickens tells us "a few of the poor children were crying, but otherwise the universal cheerfulness was amazing." (Mormons remain amazingly cheerful. Not to traffic in stereotypes, but a 2012 Gallup survey put LDS members at the top of the heap in the happiness category.) He did express a little concern over the "happy delusions they are laboring under." He told a Mormon agent on board, "It is surprising to me that these people are all so cheery, and make so little of the immense distance." If the Hughes family could see what lay ahead of them over the immense distance (three thousand nautical miles to New York and another two thousand miles overland in round figures), they wouldn't have been in such good spirits. But while hindsight is 20/20, foresight is blind.

As a writer, Dickens especially loved watching the devotion the Mormons put into penning missives. He watched with approval before leaving the ship cabins to interview the captain. When he returned, they were still at it: "Surely an extraordinary people in their power of self-abstraction. All the former letter-writers were still writing calmly and many more letter-writers had broken out in my absence." Although three-year-old Mattie wouldn't have been able to do more than scribble, she grew up to be a voluble letter-writer. Her grown-up letters to her husband, which she would write from exile in England, make for fascinating reading.

Charming as he found the mass of orderly, cheerful, letter-writing Latter-day Saints, Dickens found it "absurd" that the majority were "polygamically possessed." Dickens did not leave port with the Mormons, having satisfied his curiosity that the terrible reputation they had among his fellow countrymen was—for the most part—undeserved.

SHIPBOARD REALITY TURNED MISERABLE pretty quickly. A trip on an emigrant ship crossing the Atlantic was no Carnival cruise. Passengers were packed chock-a-block, four to six on a six-foot-square berth, their bags and cases squeezed into the aisles. The buffet was a starchy spread of biscuits, potatoes and bread. And this was not just any bread; this was a special shipboard variety made by grinding stale leftovers and rebaking it with a bit of fresh flour, sugar and baking powder. Yum, right? At least they got stinky water to wash it all down. A ship's casks were used interchangeably for water, turpentine, vinegar and oil.

All things considered, it may not have been entirely bad that each adult got only seven pounds of this delightful fare per week. And yet it apparently was. Ship crews were infamous for using extra rations to buy sex from women passengers. (Certainly, *that* never happened on the *Mormon* ships.)

Happier events that certainly did happen were shipboard weddings. The Mormons were nothing if not enthusiastic marriers. In addition to the exchanging of vows, the bride would be hoisted up the mast, and her groom would be plunked onto a chair and carried around on the deck. Imagine the hilarity!

And lordy, the passengers surely needed some hilarity now and again. A wedding would be a welcome break, but then it was back to the monotony of endless sea broken up by the terror of a storm or dread of shipwreck—followed by more endless sea.

The Hughes family disembarked into the bustle and grime of New York City, where they got stuck when Peter Hughes fell ill, too ill to work. To keep her family from starving, Elizabeth sewed men's neckwear. That kind of work paid for only the worst housing in New York City and not for long. To complicate life further, Elizabeth gave birth during this time. Mary and Mattie had a new baby sister, Annie Lloyd Hughes. There was no way Elizabeth could sew enough neckties to keep a roof over their heads.

Erastus Snow to the rescue! Erastus was one of the Latter-day Saints' illustrious Quorum of the Twelve Apostles who just happened to be on a mission to the East Coast at the time of the Hughes family's plight. He was sent from Utah back east to make converts and also shepherd the already converted to Brigham Young's Kingdom of God. Erastus offered Peter and Elizabeth a loan from the Emigrating Fund to join other Saints leaving New York. Never mind Peter's poor health; desperate times call for desperate measures. The family boarded a train with other Saints Erastus had rounded up. From New York, they headed west.

It was not a great time to be traveling by train. It was not a great time, period. The Civil War had broken out. Union troops were on the move, jostling with Mormons on the train. For emigrants from Wales, the Civil War must have seemed perplexing but not their personal concern. They were bound for Zion. The war over slavery was for others to fight.

Once the Mormons arrived in Illinois, they boarded a river steamboat to Hannibal, Missouri, where Mark Twain grew up. Twain wasn't remotely famous yet. Until the Civil War, he'd been the pilot of a steamer like the one the Hugheses were traveling on. Then he spent an entire two weeks in the Confederate army before taking off on a stagecoach for Nevada Territory with his brother Orion. They would make a memorable stop at Utah along the way.

After stocking up on food in Hannibal, the Hughes family and fellow Mormons rode another train across Missouri and then boarded a second river steamboat at St. Joseph, Missouri. Finally, they steamed into Florence, Nebraska, where the Joseph Horne Company church wagon train was being organized.

First things first: these city-slicker Londoners and Welsh coal miners got a crash course in how to drive a team of oxen. Nebraskan bystanders yukked it up watching the foreigners struggling to grab an animal by its horns or tail, wrangling a yoke into place, all while shouting in weird accents. The oxen, for their part, were just confused.

Once the oxen got yoked up, six hundred adults, plus their children and possessions, left with fifty-six wagons. They departed Florence in July 1861 for a one-thousand-mile overland trek. If you're old enough to remember Westerns on TV or have ever tuned into one of the all-Western-all-the-time rerun stations, your mind's eye may call up an image of a covered Conestoga wagon with a woman riding in front. She's wearing lipstick and blusher. Her bodice stretches tight across a bullet bra. If the producers were going for realism, her bonnet may be flopping just a tad. Rattling around behind her is the family's beloved wooden trunk from the old country and maybe even a piano.

That's not how it was.

Elizabeth Hughes walked the entire way. From Nebraska to Utah. One thousand miles. Five to twenty miles a day, fifteen on average. Elizabeth's shoes fell apart. She tied them to her feet with rags. For much of the journey, she carried baby Annie, too, feeding her as she walked. What else could she do? And it was hot. Our good anthropologist Sir Richard F. Burton described the air "like the breath of a furnace…dust-pillars and mirage were the only moving objects on the plain."

With little or no means to wash clothes, Elizabeth's blouse would have been sweat-stained, dust-coated and wrinkled. Don't forget that an adult woman's clothing at the time weighed thirty-seven pounds. Bras hadn't even been invented yet, much less the 1950s bullet style. And makeup? Nope. No way.

Mark Twain and his brother were traveling west on a stagecoach at the same time as the John Horne Company. Twain described the people on a Mormon wagon train: "Coarse and sad-looking.…Dusty and uncombed, hatless, bonnetless and ragged and they did look so tired." These folks had come a long way from the fresh-faced letter writers Dickens described.

As for the contents of their wagon, Elizabeth and Peter were allowed fifty pounds of personal belongings each. That's the same weight United Airlines allows per passenger on international flights. The Hugheses weren't toting any heavy wooden heirlooms, that's for sure. Mattie's father, Peter, who was too sick to walk, lay wedged among the belongings of his and ten other families, or he may have been allowed a ride in the hospital wagon. Mattie and Mary walked beside their mother or hung off the wagon's sides when they couldn't keep up.

The travelers fueled up for each day of walking with a "breakfast composed of various abominations, especially cakes of flour and grease, molasses and dirt, disposed in pretty equal parts." At least, that's how Ruffian Dick described it, and he should know, having been served up a plate as part of his research. If the cows didn't die, there would be fresh milk. Some days, they ate antelope or hares if the men were good shots. This game was cooked over a fire of buffalo chips (dried bison turds), which, ironically, may have given off a relatively nice aroma, particularly among six hundred people who walked all day in the hot sun and got to bathe only every two weeks. Bison eat grass, so that's what their dung smells like when it's burning—kind of pleasant, actually. Reportedly.

The veggies they ate included whatever weeds they pulled along the way. Lamb's quarters and mallow, the scourge of today's gardens and lawns, made a prairie salad. For fruit, they scrounged for wild grapes, currants and gooseberries, which taste sweet, sour and acidic. Their tannins make your mouth pucker, which probably made the kids laugh.

So, maybe not every second was hell. In the evenings, the travelers danced to violins. Burton wrote: "The 'fiddle' was a favorite instrument with Mr. Joseph Smith as the harp with [biblical King] David; the Mormons, therefore, at the insistence of their prophet, are not a little addicted to the use of the bow."

While the fiddles were trilling in the evening, daytime brought the creak of the wagons and the music of the prairie. The travelers heard the bell-like chirrups of meadowlarks, the clipped peets of plovers, the stutters and whistles of western bluebirds and the far less melodious squawks of magpies—not to mention the hum of mosquitos. Anthropologist Burton (Ruffian Dick) complained of the "atrocity of the mosquitos" he had to swat away all day as part of his research.

The landscape they traversed ranged from grass-bestubbled prairie to otherworldly rock outcroppings. The route started out passing small farms and tiny settlements. Eventually, they splashed through La Grande Platte, which Burton described as "the dreariest of rivers," a statement as true now as then. Anyone who has ever driven I-80 across the grasslands of Nebraska complains of the boredom, so imagine walking it! It's just mile after mile of monotonous grass and sage, occasionally ripped by gullies and "criks." Then, out of nowhere, Chimney Rock juts up from the plains. To a four-year-old from Wales, it would have resembled nothing so much as the handle of a spoon standing up from a bowl of porridge. It marked the halfway point, more or less.

Mattie and Mary must have clapped their little hands in delight when they saw Wyoming's prairie dog villages. Thousands of cute rodents popped up out of holes, joggling their little heads to and fro before popping back down.

Chimney Rock. *By permission, Utah State Historical Society.*

The girls would have been entertained by rabbits' antics, first cottontails and then, farther west, jackrabbits. Less entertaining were the rattlesnakes.

The John Horne Company passed workers installing telegraph poles. The idea of instantaneous communication across a continent must have seemed crazy and miraculous to the Victorians (like baby boomers view the internet). Even so, Morse code required too many expensive dots and dashes to share the details of frontier life with friends and family separated by distance and circumstances. Mormons kept writing their letters, while the new-fangled telegraph promised to keep them up to date with national events, the war and news of births and deaths once they got to far-flung Utah.

But let's not get distracted in romanticism. The trek was mostly hell.

Baby Annie died along the way.

Bacterial infections killed pioneers of all ages. Mountain fever infected people through tick bites. Typhoid invaded bodies through fecal-contaminated food. So did dysentery, as every gen-Xer or millennial knows, thanks to playing *Oregon Trail*. The medicines in the hospital wagon—opium, citric acid, green tea and Warburg's Drops (a concoction of quinine, rhubarb, saffron, fennel, chalk and myrrh)—were useless against salmonella, rickettsia and shigella. Antibiotics and effective insecticides lay almost one hundred years in the future.

The Hughes family wrapped Annie's tiny body and left her in a shallow grave covered by a pile of stones. The stones were small hope to deter animals from digging up the remains. The Hugheses were hardly alone in their grief. Thirty-three in their company died along the way.

And yet they kept walking.

By mid-September, the company arrived in Utah, the "Holy Valley of the West." The immigrants saw what Burton described as "this lovely panorama of green and azure and gold this land, fresh as it were from the hands of God." The city slowly came into sight. "Before them lay the lovely valley of the Great Salt Lake, seeming to their weary eyes a very paradise of rest and contentment," wrote the anti-Mormon propagandist Jennie Anderson Froiseth in one of her kinder passages. "In the distance the briny waters of the lake glistened brightly in the sunlight. Many heartfelt prayers of gratitude went up to the Father above for bringing them safely to this peaceful harbor." The dust kicked up by their wagons rose like a smoke column, announcing their approach to the citizens of Salt Lake City, who got ready to celebrate. Every arrival was a party.

The custom was for the filthy immigrants to bathe and put on clean clothes before entering the city. The men would even shave. They would

Every wagon train arrival sparked a celebration. *Library of Congress, LC-USZ62-113102.*

arrive in Zion clean and singing hymns. On September 13, 1861, Elizabeth, Peter, Mary and Mattie Hughes did just that.

As they entered Salt Lake City, there would have been celebratory "sobs and tears, laughter and congratulations, psalms and hysterics....The children dance, the strong men cheer and shout....Nervous women, broken with fatigue and hope deferred, scream and faint; that the ignorant should fondly believe that the 'spirit of God' pervades the very atmosphere," as Burton put it.

Three days later, Peter Hughes was dead.

LIFE WENT ON. THE church allotted the widow Elizabeth one and one-quarter acre of land for her and the two girls. At first, they lived in a dugout (that's a hole in the ground plus a roof). Rough-and-ready architecture was the norm. In 1864, the *Atlantic* magazine described the Mormons' first-things-first ethos: "The fields are billowing over with dense, golden grain, the cattle are wallowing in emerald lakes of juicy grass, the barns are substantial, the family-windmill buzzes merrily on its well-oiled pivot...but the house is desolate."

Before the year was out, Elizabeth had married the widower James Patten Paul. Her haste is to be forgiven. In those days, whether a woman lived in polygamous Utah or anywhere else, survival required marriage, at least for those in the working classes.

The couple built a grey-blue adobe house, and like most in Salt Lake at the time, they planted a garden and raised pigs. Their marriage, like the vast majority of Mormon marriages, stayed monogamous. James Paul had four sons of his own. Together, Elizabeth and James had five more children, a total of eleven, and that went about as well as you'd expect. Elizabeth said to her husband James: "Your children and my children are abusing our children."

Sibling rivalry notwithstanding, Mattie had a happy childhood. Compared to the dirty winds of Wales, the air in Utah was, in anthropologist Burton's words, "of exceeding purity and tenuity." The Latter-day Saints and their oxen had dug ditches to pull water from the canyons to the desert city. There, it watered apple trees, peach trees, maize and sorghum. Irrigated gardens grew a harvest of potatoes, onions, cabbages, cucumbers, tomatoes and wheat. They also grew flowers—roses, geraniums, tansies and nasturtiums. Today's Salt Lake City isn't so agricultural, but folk remain profligate with the posies.

The Salt Lake City business district of Mattie's time offered a bakery, a butcher shop, a blacksmith, a hardware store, shoe stores, a tailor, a grocery market, furniture shops and even liquor stores. As part of his field research, Burton hopped into Salt Lake stores, which he found to be "far superior, in all points, to the shops in an English country town." As one would expect in a place that practices polygamy, "the merchants are careful to keep on hand a large stock of fancy goods, millinery, and other feminine adornments."

When little Mattie had a birthday, it's possible James and Elizabeth took her to the city's ice cream parlor, where a cold cone could be had for twenty-five cents. (That would be about five dollars today—maybe eight.)

She could entertain herself with books from the city's public library. Neighbors also put on "theatricals" for each other. In the winter, the Mormons went on sleigh rides. And just like they did on the prairie, they loved dancing to the fiddle. Sir Burton/Ruffian Dick joked that, to the Latter-day Saints, "Dancing seems to be considered an edifying enterprise." He found the Mormons of 1860s Salt Lake City to be regular party animals all around. One bash he attended went on for "thirteen successive mortal hours—it shows a solid power of enduring enjoyments!"

The city was rife with news hounds, too. Burton said, "Mormonism, so far from despising the powers of pica, has a more than ordinary respect for them." (Their respect for the pica left behind a treasure trove for historians. The J. Willard Marriott Library at the University of Utah has put 170 years' worth online. In the 1800s, there were seventy newspapers published in Utah; today, there are forty-seven, with ten times the population.) One of the city's respected newspapers, the *Woman's Exponent*, employed teenage Mattie Paul Hughes as a typesetter. This was her second career, after she'd given up on becoming a schoolteacher. Typesetting funded her college education.

Presiding over everything was Second Prophet Brigham Young. The handsome, charming and lecherous founder of the Church of Jesus Christ of Latter-day Saints, Joseph Smith, had died years before. It was the portly pragmatist Brigham Young who went public with the polygamy thing and transplanted the entire Mormon shebang to Utah.

There, it was Young who built, as Twain's wit put it, a "city of 15,000 inhabitants with no loafers perceptible in it, and no visible drunkards or noisy people." (It's a little different nowadays but not that much.) The first thing Young did was stick his cane into the ground and proclaim, "Here will be the Temple of our God"—or so the story goes. He was referring to his planned neo-Gothic temple, whose grandiosity presides over Salt Lake City to this day. In 1900, the *Atlantic* magazine called the temple "mysterious,

The Salt Lake Temple took forty years to build. *Library of Congress, LC-USZ62-36477.*

repellent, yet fascinating, a Gregorian chant done in deathless granite," which is one way to look at it.

(At the moment, from 2020 to 2026 or so, the temple is shrouded in scaffolding and plastic, as contractors are digging deep beneath the structure to install a base isolation system to protect it from God's earthquakes.)

Anyway, the temple was still just a hole in the ground when Mattie was growing up. It would take forty years to finish. That's pretty fast, historically speaking. Notre Dame took almost two hundred years to complete, and Winchester Cathedral took four hundred years to build. In the meantime, the Saints had their turtle-shaped tabernacle for large meetings and musical concerts and a simple two-story "Endowment House" for all those rituals that would eventually be done in the temple, like weddings—lots of weddings.

Down the street from the tabernacle and temple-under-construction was Brigham Young's prodigiously gabled (twenty in all) Lion House, where a dozen-plus of his wives lived with their many, many children. It was named after the lion statue that still presides over the front door.

While the Second Prophet was not the unbridled lothario the First Prophet was, he was no slouch in the wives department. He had even more wives than he could fit into the Lion House. Historians count somewhere between sixteen and forty wives total, depending on how you define *wife*. But at the Beehive House, Bill the tour guide says Brigham had fifty-six wives. Let's go with that. Some, he just supported financially. But he was obviously no celibate. According to the official tally of the LDS Church, he "begat" fifty-six children by sixteen wives.

Young's Utah was firmly founded on the public acknowledgement and theology of polygamy. Victorian moralists hither and yon were aghast— aghast I tell you! They were so aghast that they couldn't read enough about it, tut-tutting all the while, rather like our own obsession with the successive wives and husbands of the rich and famous. Mark Twain made fun of the fascination: "Our stay in Salt Lake City amounted to only two days, and therefore we had no time to make the customary inquisition into the workings of polygamy and get up the usual statistics and deductions preparatory to calling the attention of the nation at large once more to the matter." Nevertheless, he wrote, "We felt a curiosity to ask every child how many mothers it had."

Among the Victorian-era Mormons of Utah, a few practiced polygamy, more wished to but couldn't afford it and still others thought it was a great idea for *other* people. It was not all about men wanting extra wives and first wives saying no. Some men were content with one wife, and some women really wished their husband would take another. Different strokes for different folks.

This was the culture in which Mattie Paul Hughes grew up, graduated from medical school and became the well-respected Dr. Martha Paul Hughes. She was smart and pretty and pursued by young men who promised to make her their one and only. Nevertheless, Mattie jumped at the chance to marry a much older man who already had three wives. Why?

To understand this, let's take a deeper dive into the world of Victorian sex. If you still imagine great-great-great-grandma's generation as one of strait-laced prudes, strap in. The 1800s were full of adultery, prostitution, porn, "free love" and sex communes. The Mormon polygamists argued that all things considered, their system was the more progressive. If anything, polygamists claimed, they were the better strait-laced prudes, and their critics were hypocrites.

They weren't wrong.

5

DOWN AND DIRTY

Victorian Prostitution and Adultery

Ladies of negotiable affections were ubiquitous in the nineteenth century. The Cult of True Womanhood didn't promote abstinence or sexual morality as you probably guessed it wouldn't. It became, instead, by accident or design, effective marketing for the commercialization of sex. Dutiful husband with dastardly desires and a dainty wife meets single woman with few means of making an independent living.

SEX WORK WAS NOTHING new. It flourished in the prior century. Benjamin Franklin related his personal experience in the 1700s: "In the meantime, that hard-to-be-governed passion of youth hurried me frequently into intrigues with low women that fell in my way, which were attended with some expense and great inconvenience."

But demand for paid sex went off the charts in the 1800s, when Victorian culture convinced men to continue with "intrigues with low women" well beyond the "passion of youth." Husbands took seriously the charge to find an outlet for carnal desires that protected their wives' True Womanhood. The sex industry was christened a "necessary evil."

The system was outrageously classist. "Gentlemen" visited bordellos with the idea of protecting the virtue of "innocent" women. By *innocent*, they meant the women of their own class. Such a gentleman would not hesitate to pay to "ruin" (that's their word) a poor and desperate virgin. Indeed, he might pay extra for the privilege. Bordellos received police protection. "If it

Victorian men frequently sought ladies of negotiable affections. *iStock.*

were not for such as these, your wives and daughters would not be safe," said one brothel-keeper to government inspectors.

Brothel owners, typically women madams, were respected members of their communities. Pimps, on the other hand, were not. Male procurers were dubbed "secretaries" or "men of fancy dress and patent leather shoes." (Should we readopt that title?)

"Wages" ran the gamut, and likewise, prices ranged from the outrageously expensive to bargain basement. On fashionable Fifth Avenue in New York, the wealthiest of the wealthy kept fancy consorts in luxurious mansions. The wealthy but not-quite-*that*-wealthy john could instead inquire of an escort service. When a woman was available, the madam would invite these men to "call and try on her gloves." Then the man would be expected to treat the woman to dinner and dancing before ultimately getting what he paid for. A *Gentleman's Guide* was published to help men find sex in unfamiliar cities, a *Fodor's* for the frisky.

Wealthy men and top-flight madams organized by-invitation-only balls. They would reserve a pleasant venue and hire a good band and high-class caterer. They were rather like a formal wedding reception today—at least at the outset, not so much as the night wore on. The most prolific pornographer of the era (or any era, for that matter), "Walter," described such a ball in *My Secret Life*:

> *The men paid for their suppers, and each paid also for a lady....The men were all in evening clothes, the women beautifully dressed, and décolleté.... No introductions were needed, any man asked any woman to dance, altho [sic], to avoid jealousy, that needed some discretion; and the women did not hesitate to ask the men to dance with them. Everything in fact was free and easy, but not immodest, until after supper, when it got more free and easy. Then the dancing became romping, and concupiscence asserted itself....As I danced with one woman, the aroma from her naked bosom and armpits enervated me. (Etc.)*

Lower on the scale were regular parlor houses. The top-hatted, cravat-wearing john who didn't snag an invite to a private ball could nevertheless sit on a brocade couch, listen to a skilled pianist and singer and sip champagne before taking a silk-swathed woman to a private chamber. More affordable brothels offered much the same, but the chairs were stained, the pianist was less skilled and the bubbly was beer instead of champagne. Near the bottom were "cribs," where working men could rent a woman's bed and body for just enough minutes to get the job done (three, by some reports, if the sex worker was especially skilled).

At the very bottom was the woman with no bed who lifted her skirts for a penny in an alleyway. "Walter" again said (because he enjoyed the low-down as well as the high-flown): "I shagged many of all sorts and sizes, many of them poor creatures, others plump, fine, strong healthy women whom I was surprised took the small sum for their professional exertions."

And let's not forget the poor women who didn't even get the smallest sum. Plantation owners would "protect" the delicate white belles by exploiting enslaved women who were definitely not prostitutes but had no way to refuse their masters.

A street walker, the lowest rung of sex work. *Library of Congress, LC-USZC4-8773.*

SOCIAL REFORMERS, USUALLY UPPER-CLASS women, crusaded to rescue the "fallen women" on the streets and in the brothels. In Victorian culture, a single woman who lost her virginity before marriage was honor bound to accept the only profession available to a "ruined" woman. This was where the Victorians veered sharply from the attitudes of earlier eras. Prior to the 1800s, a female "sinner" could be forgiven by the community and go on to marry and have a regular life. The Cult of True Womanhood placed women on such a high moral pedestal that once a woman had fallen off, her virtue was shattered forever. In the Victorian world, there were two kinds of women: angels and whores—and nobody in between. But there was only one kind of man.

Others thought it wiser just to accept that "[h]ouses of prostitution doubtless *must* exist" (emphasis added), in the words of a select committee as reported by the *New York Tribune* and repeated with opprobrium by the Mormon *Deseret News*:

> *Whatever may be the odium incurred by the suggestion among honest people who have not mingled with the world, who are ignorant of its passions and of their fatal effects, the Committee are willing to take it upon themselves in earnestly recommending to the Legislature the regulating of, or if the word be not deemed offensive, the licensing of prostitution....If anybody's conscience can be soothed, his moral doubts be assuaged, by dropping the word "license" and using the word "regulation," the Committee have no earthly objections.*

Still others focused on disease prevention. Medical authorities inspected sex workers for syphilis and gonorrhea. As there was no cure for these venereal diseases, doctors' concern was not the health of the sex workers, it was for the protection of johns and their wives.

Salt Lake City's approach was to use periodic arrests and small fines as de facto licensing, although Mormons insisted only gentiles patronized their city's "houses of ill fame." For the Latter-day Saints, de facto licensure held a special appeal. When federal agents made trouble for polygamists, it was easy enough to expose their hypocrisy by entrapping a few G-men in a brothel raid. One assistant U.S. attorney was caught this way, but he got off, being a U.S. attorney and all.

Landlords were fond of bordellos, too, since madams paid the highest rents. Over the objections of a minority of directors, the Brigham Young Company rented property to Madam Ada Wilson for a sumptuous brothel she called the Palace. Ada showed her appreciation by inviting prominent church leaders to her grand opening. Some attended. They may have been clueless, merely curious or potential customers. Who knows?

After the turn of the century, Salt Lake City went all in on de jure licensure, creating a fenced-in district called the Stockade in 1907. The city's sex workers were confined under the supervision of Madam Dora Topham. The women held licenses and received regular health inspections from doctors. This legal and regulated system lasted only three years before the Civic Betterment League got it closed down, but the LDS Church continued to rent real estate to brothel operators until 1941—for the gentiles, of course.

"FALLEN WOMEN" WERE THE supply that met the demand of the nineteenth-century sex industry. How exactly did a woman fall into sex work? What transformed so many angels into so many whores?

Gosh, it was easy—almost inescapable. It was not necessary to actually engage in commercial sex or any kind of sex to be considered a prostitute. Rule number one: to avoid being labeled a whore, never ever step across the threshold of a tavern for any reason. Rule number two: don't sell flowers; everybody knows selling flowers is a front for prostitution, even if you really do just sell flowers. There were many other rules, too. A virtuous woman had to be super careful not to turn her head on the street, look in shop windows, swing her arms, "hustle" across an intersection, pull on gloves in public or suck on the handle of her parasol. OK, that last one kind of makes sense.

Dr. Martha Hughes Cannon, the wife of eminent LDS Church leader Angus Cannon, a future Utah state senator, experienced this judgmentalism herself. After the birth of her first child, she exiled herself and their child to Europe to protect Angus from prosecution for polygamy. She wrote home: "It is an <u>absolute fact</u> that a woman can't travel here in Europe with a baby, unless accompanied by her husband, without having the child branded with illegitimacy and herself looked upon as one who has submitted herself to prostitution." A woman carrying a baby outside the presence of her husband was certainly the everyday way of things in polygamous Utah, but Mattie would have encountered the same judgment traveling in other parts of the United States.

The fact that there were more women labeled prostitutes than there were actual prostitutes does not mean sex work wasn't a common vocation for women. It was for many reasons, all based on human instinct for survival in a world that refused to pay fair wages to husbandless women. Susan B. Anthony was a rare voice of common sense when she pointed to the obvious motivation: poverty. "Nightly, as weary and worn from her day's toil she wends her way through the dark alleys to her still darker abode, where only cold and hunger await her, she sees on every side and at every turn the gilded hand of vice and crime outstretched." You've got to love how the Victorians described things. In a fit of rational problem-solving, Susan B. suggested that the way to prevent women from falling into paid sex work was to pay them fairly for non–sex work. What an idea!

While the primary motivator pushing women into the sex industry was a misogynist economic system that forced single women and their children into destitution and homelessness, a few women chose sex work for other reasons. About a quarter of Victorian sex workers were game for the life.

"I went into the sporting life for business reasons and for no other. It was a way for a woman in those days to make money, and I made it," Mattie Silks, a Denver madam, told a *Rocky Mountain News* reporter on her deathbed.

AMATEUR ADULTERY WAS ANOTHER popular Victorian pastime. Not every illicit liaison had to involve a commercial transaction! Adultery was not entirely acceptable, but it was considered normal—for the husband. And man, oh, man, did society embrace the double standard. Although a gentleman would avoid bragging about his adulterous affairs in polite society, his friends would not think less of him as long as his behavior was discreet and he disclosed his shenanigans only in the males-only privacy of the cigar lounge.

Not only was the double standard culturally accepted, it was also enshrined into law. Should a wife discover her husband was unfaithful, she was expected to forgive him. If a man discovered his wife was unfaithful, his choices were to beat her, kill her or, if he were the kindly sort, sue for divorce and take their children. A husband could divorce his wife for adultery alone. A wife, on the other hand, had to convince a judge that he had committed adultery *plus* incest, cruelty or some other crime.

Few objected, with the exception of mouthy rabble-rousers. Those included feminists like Susan B. Anthony, first woman presidential candidate Victoria Woodhull and the polygamous Mormons.

Dr. Martha Hughes Cannon opined that it was "a burning shame to the face of Christianity, where the 'mis-step' of the brother receives no severer appellation than 'wild oats,' which is soon forgotten, while his sister is branded for life and bears the burden of her misfortune alone."

Nobody exposed the era's hypocrisy with more unadulterated glee than the indomitable Victoria Woodhull. "Progress! Free Thought! Untrammeled

"Progress! Free Thought! Untrammeled Lives!" Victoria Woodhull sloganized. *Mathew B. Brady, circa 1870; Fine Arts Library, Harvard University.*

Lives!" was the slogan for her newspaper, *Woodhull & Claflin's Weekly*, which, on November 2, 1872, published a report setting forth the details of the Reverend Henry Ward Beecher's adulterous affair with Elizabeth Tilton, also known as Mrs. Theodore Tilton, the wife of the famous writer and abolitionist who had been Beecher's assistant. The report came as no big shock to Mr. Tilton, since he'd known all about it for a year or so and, being rather more liberal than other men of his era, had decided to neither beat nor divorce his wife. For the rest of the country, however, the report "burst like a bombshell," which was exactly what Victoria Woodhull intended. She sold more than one hundred thousand copies, which filled her bank account to bursting. Would you be surprised to learn that Reverend Beecher's life went on thoroughly untrammeled?

On the other hand, the bombshell trammeled Victoria's life and the life of her sister and fellow-publisher Tennessee Claflin to bits. Law enforcement read the thoroughly accurate news article about the good reverend as porn. Victoria and Tennessee were arrested for circulating an obscene newspaper through the mail. They were locked up for six months.

Eight years later, Reverend Beecher rose to the defense of fellow bad boy Grover Cleveland. Grover's behavior was much ickier than the reverend's. When he was forty years old, Grover had an "illicit acquaintance" and a "bastard child" with a widowed salesclerk named Maria Halpin, whom he had met at church. According to Halpin, the former Erie County sheriff Grover Cleveland pursued her relentlessly and "the circumstances under which my ruin was accomplished are too revolting on the part of Grover Cleveland to be made public." There's that word again—*ruin*. He overtook her "by use of force and violence and without my consent." That is, he raped her, an accusation that Grover never bothered to deny. She told him she never wanted to see him again.

Then she found out she was pregnant. Maria asked Grover to marry her to make their son legitimate (which was the default solution to pregnancy

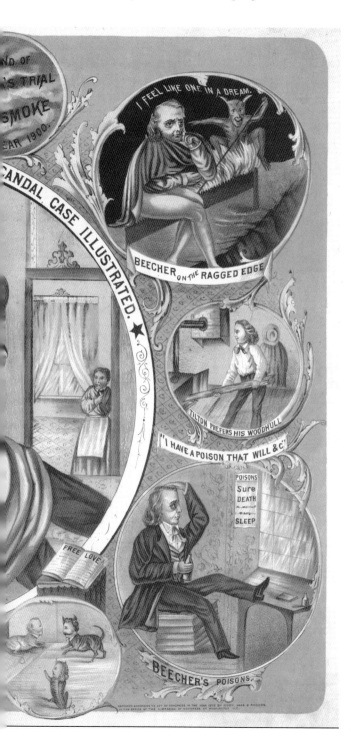

This scandal didn't affect
the adulterers too much.
*Library of Congress, LC-DIG-
pga-03156.*

by rape well into the twentieth century). Rather than do the gallant thing, old Grover lectured the mother-to-be, "What the devil are you blubbering about? You act like a baby without teeth." So, they didn't get married.

As soon as Maria's son was born, he was taken from her against her will, fostered by a local couple, returned to her a year later and then taken away again, this time to an orphanage. When Maria went to the orphanage to get him back, she was accused of being insane and committed to an asylum. Because she was not insane at all and instead maybe just a little bit drunk, the doctors released her. She found the child and hired an attorney to charge Grover with assault and kidnapping. Grover then wrote out a settlement, offering $500 for her to surrender the baby and make no more demands on him. What a guy—a whole $500! The baby did end up getting adopted by another family in Buffalo and eventually became a physician and pioneer in obstetrics and gynecology.

No harm was done to Grover, though. He went on to run for president of the United States. Supporters of Cleveland's opponent James Blaine came up with a catchy little ditty: "Ma, ma, where's my pa?" But it didn't work. Grover came out of the scandal untrammeled with no help from Maria. When asked to make a statement in support of Grover's candidacy, Maria responded, "I would rather put a bullet through my heart." Grover won the presidency and moved into the White House.

In the middle of the brou-ha-ha, Reverend Beecher asserted: "If every man…who has broken the Seventh Commandment voted for Cleveland, he would be elected by a two hundred thousand majority."

Sitting as we are now in the twenty-first century, not much has changed in the area of sexual hypocrisy of celebrity clergy and presidential candidates. Switch out the names and numbers, and Beecher's statement is as true now as it was then.

6

LITTLE WANDERERS, BABY FARMS AND THE RAGAMUFFIN RAILROAD

Orphans, street urchins, abortion, abandoned babies and infanticide were the inevitable products of the Cult of True Womanhood, seeing as how sheep gut and Madame Frain's Famous Female Mixture weren't very reliable. Paying a sex worker, supporting a mistress or taking "privileges" with an enslaved woman were more effective means of limiting the size of middle-class and upper-middle-class families. But the practices weren't contraception. Concupiscence inevitably leads to conception—just not necessarily with one's wife.

Any thoughtful reader of Dickens or history buff with an interest in the Victorian era will eventually wonder where the heck did all those orphans come from? Sure, life expectancies were shorter back then, but how did it happen that all these children had both their mothers *and* fathers die on them? And why weren't aunts and uncles or kindly Christian neighbors stepping up to foster them?

The answer is that most weren't actually orphans. Well over half of nineteenth-century "orphans" had at least one, if not both, living parents.

Mothers can and do still make the loving decision to give their child to adoptive parents. Provided there's no coercion, indirectly from the culture or directly by another person, the decision to place a child up for adoption can work out well. Women today are free to choose single motherhood, but that was not a respectable choice for great-great-great-grandma—or even grandma. Into the 1980s, the default for single moms was to place their babies up for adoption, hence all the DNA shockers delivered today courtesy of 23andMe.

Sometimes, nineteenth-century widower fathers left their children in orphanages because they couldn't figure out how to both work and watch their children. A larger group of orphans, street urchins and abandoned babies were born of "ruined" servants and sex workers, who faced the exact same dilemma.

Childcare options for single mothers were bleak. Few fathers accepted responsibility, since, after all, one attraction to paying a sex worker or exploiting a servant was to avoid responsibility in the first place. Also, paternity was impossible to prove. In England, they didn't even try. English law explicitly protected men from taking responsibility for children conceived outside their marriage. As for extended family, the parents and siblings of fallen women felt more shame than responsibility. The last thing they wanted was a product of sin living in their home. What would the neighbors think?

In the first half of the century, the county poorhouse was a last resort for impoverished mothers. It was filled with paupers, alcoholics, the mentally ill and elderly folks waiting to die. Poorhouses were deliberately designed to be places of wretched misery and humiliation under the philosophy that the worse they were, the harder people would work to stay out of them. And single mothers really did work hard to stay out of them. Sometimes, however, there was just no avoiding it. A pregnant woman can sleep in the gutter, but what happens when her water breaks? The county-funded poorhouse came to serve as a maternity ward. By the mid-1800s, about a third of poorhouse residents were babies and children.

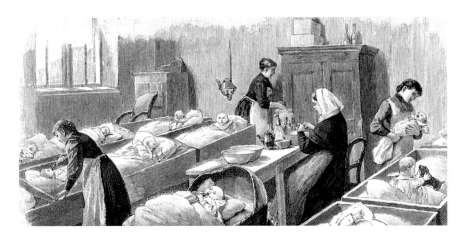

Drugging newborns for profit at a "baby farm." *iStock.*

The poorhouse was a notoriously rotten place to raise kids, so the free market stepped in to solve the predicament. For-profit private businesses called "baby farms" promised to find adoptive homes for these children—for a fee, of course. Desperate to avoid the poorhouse, a soiled dove saved her pennies in the hope that the baby farmer would find a nice married couple to adopt her baby. Maximizing profit being a matter of taking in revenue in one column while minimizing costs in another, baby farmers made the business decision to limit spending. If an infant didn't get adopted right away, the baby farmer allowed infection and starvation to take their natural course. If the starving, diaper-rash-afflicted baby cried too much, the baby farmer fed it a soothing tonic officially named Godfrey's cordial and commonly known as "mother's helper." We call it opium. A generous dose had the dual benefit of quieting the child and hastening its death, freeing up the crib for another fee.

It was a gruesome world.

A LESS GRUESOME OPTION for single mothers was to bear the shame, keep their children and just get along as best they could. That meant leaving the kids to their own devices while the mother worked. Whether a single mom was sewing buttons, selling sex or emptying a rich lady's excrement from her bedpan, keeping a watchful eye on the children was an impossibility if she was going to put porridge in their bowls and coal in their stove.

It's estimated that in 1849, there were ten thousand vagrant children running about New York City. All cities had thousands of children living on the streets. These children were called waifs, guttersnipes, ragamuffins, wayward children, vagabonds, friendless children, fatherless children, street Arabs (it was a racist era, too), luckless children, little wanderers, urchins and little laborers.

Little laborers helped their mothers by searching the docks and alleys for bits of coal that dropped out of trucks. They'd drag sacks of it home to fuel the family's cook stove or heat the tenement. Other kids made money shining shoes, hawking newspapers and selling candy and flowers. Horatio Alger fantasies notwithstanding, these children were not viewed as enterprising young entrepreneurs. Their middle-class customer base considered them nuisances. Remember the infamous Squeegee Boys of Rudy Giuliani's 1990s New York or the gum peddlers on Mexican beaches? That's how they were seen.

SOMETHING HAD TO CHANGE. Apparently out of the question was allowing women to take good-paying jobs and requiring fathers to support their offspring. The only people who thought those were good ideas were crazy feminists and the polygamous Mormons. Gentiles in the greater United States had other ideas: train rides and orphanages.

Train rides were the first scheme. A surplus of poor children in eastern cities met a scarcity of labor on middle western farms. *Ta da*! "Placing out" city kids to farms was the brainchild of Charles Loring Brace, an idealistic New York City missionary. He devoted his life to saving children from moral degradation and destitution, having concluded that saving their parents was "well-nigh hopeless."

His program and its imitators came to be known as the orphan trains. It's a cute moniker but is misleading, since half the kids weren't orphans. Ragamuffin railroad would be more accurate. From 1854 to 1929, approximately two hundred thousand destitute children rode trains west to become farmhands, unskilled laborers and housekeepers. They came from asylums, prisons and tenements. Some penniless parents relinquished their children voluntarily, imagining they were giving their kids wholesome lives of fulfilling work in the great outdoors. And sometimes, that's what the kids got—but not always.

In August 1882, the Children's Home Society of New York announced it was bringing a "company of boys" to the little town of St. James in the flat and fertile farm country of south-central Minnesota. The announcement in the newspaper read: "Applicants are expected to treat the children as their own in the matter of schooling and training." A committee was supposed to screen applicants for worthiness to be employer-parents of these little wanderers from New York City, which shouldn't have been too hard, since there were only twelve applicants in a small town where everybody knew everyone else.

Unfortunately, the committee's screening process, as it turns out, was not all it was cracked up to be. Reports of drunken brutes and the like adopting innocent children made their way to a certain Congregational minister by the name of Hastings Hornell Hart, a renowned penologist. (That means he was a prison reformer! Get your mind out of the good reverend's trousers!) Reverend Hart happened to be the secretary of the Minnesota State Board of Correction and Charity, and he went south to St. James to investigate. In 1884, he personally witnessed the emptying of another train car full of little laborers, waifs and urchins. Let's just say he was not impressed. He reported back to the Board of Correction and Charity that locals were afraid to

Orphan trains took children "out west," even if they weren't orphans. *iStock*.

oppose any applicants, being more concerned about not making enemies for themselves than protecting children from exploitation and abuse.

In spite of the system's loosey-goosey structure, many kids from the ragamuffin railroad turned out fine. The ones taken from abusive homes back in New York were often (albeit not always) grateful to be given a new life out west. Many of the families who adopted these children took seriously their pledge to "treat them as their own in the matter of schooling." A few of the kids even went to college and on to professional careers. Two became governors. Andrew Burke, taken off a train in Indiana, grew up to be elected the second governor of North Dakota. John Green Brady, also taken off a train in Indiana, became a Presbyterian minister, moved to Alaska and served as the territorial governor for three terms.

THE NEXT BIG IDEA was orphanages, poorhouses made exclusively for children. Taxpayers still clung to the belief that humiliating and degrading poverty-stricken adults was a money-saver. But punishing innocent children? Softer hearts convinced penny-pinchers this was both cruel and, more importantly, counterproductive. By providing no schooling in an environment filled with drunks and ne'er-do-wells, poorhouses were turning children into exactly the kind of drags on the budget local governments were punishing their parents for being.

Orphanages seemed like a perfect solution. (For white children anyway. Black children weren't permitted in orphanages or on orphan trains.) The idea took off fast. In the last quarter of the nineteenth century, orphanages were built right and left. By 1877, the United States had 208 orphan asylums. In spite of the bad reputations they came to have, orphanages were an enlightened approach for the time. In big brick edifices with sprawling yards, children got nutritious food, secular education, religious instruction and medical care.

There was another perceived benefit: family disruption. The Victorians believed children did best when separated from parents with a poor work ethic. It didn't matter if the mother was a spurned mistress, ruined servant or even a Civil War widow, of which there was a great surplus in the second half of the century. Do-gooders wanted to give poor children a fresh start if not out west, then at an orphanage.

And perhaps strangely—perhaps not—some birth parents agreed. Poor parents worked mightily to keep out of the poorhouse, but many were eager to drop off their children at the orphanage. They saw it as a kind of free boarding school, which it sort of was. By the end of the century, four babies per day were being left at the door of Bellevue Hospital, and the same was happening at foundling hospitals elsewhere.

THE POINT ISN'T THAT baby farms, poorhouses, orphan trains and orphanages were good or bad (although baby farms and poorhouses were most definitely bad). The point is they were *necessary*. Abandoned infants and street urchins were the inevitable product of an era without effective contraception and a culture that barred women from well-paying employment while promoting female chastity and winking at sex work and male adultery.

Concupiscence leads to conception, just not necessarily with one's wife—unless it does. That was the Mormon affront. They exposed the hypocrisy of gentile culture and recommended a different approach—a shocking system. Polygamy, they argued, was the biblical answer. Polygamists didn't abandon their children.

7

POLYGAMY, HYPOCRISY AND PRESIDENTIAL PROMISCUITY

Hypocrisy didn't bother great-great-great-grandma's generation any more than it does ours. Polygamous Mormons could natter all the live-long day that polygamy was more virtuous than adultery (and trust me, they did), but the gentiles didn't get it. They were shocked! Shocked I tell you! Horrified! Scandalized by the goings-on in Utah! *Read all about it*!

By 1852, Brigham Young was done sneaking around. His polygamous system was loud and proud. It was not only out in the open, it was also ritualized. He wasn't going to lie like Joseph Smith. He was going to boast. The principle was not unchaste, it was more chaste! Polygamy was faithful and, above all, godly! LDS apostle Orson Pratt specifically argued that polygamy was the solution to adultery and prostitution (faithfulness to one wife was apparently too preposterous to contemplate). The gentiles "cry out" against polygamy, he protested, "but they can swallow down comparatively easily, without scarcely uttering a groan, the polluted, wretched, most filthy stinks of iniquity which prevail to an alarming extent in all large towns, cities, and seaports, among gentile nations."

LDS church leaders promoted polygamy as a way of freeing women from the lusts of men (for a few days at a time, anyhow), making them wives and mothers with homes of their own and respectable social positions. Mormon women pretty much agreed. LDS feminist leader and plural wife Eliza Snow exclaimed in a speech: "Where else, on Earth, is female virtue held so sacred, and where so bravely defended? Facts answer, NOWHERE!"

Mormons didn't reject the Cult of True Womanhood; they embraced it and then molded it into something entirely their own.

By this time, polyandry was out. A Mormon woman could have only one living husband on Earth and one celestial husband in the hereafter. Mormon women did not object, at least not so that anybody noticed. Since freeing women from the *demands* of men was never part of the deal and considering all the chores wives were (and are) expected to do for their husbands—cooking, cleaning, clothes washing, mending, childbearing, child tending and so on—it's hard to imagine very many women wanting two or more husbands. They were "true women," pure, chaste and faithful to one husband each.

GENTILES "FIND FAULT WITH us," Mormon apostle John Tayler complained, "for having more wives and children than they, and for preserving purity and chastity in our midst, and they would introduce infamies among us."

In 1855, infamy waltzed into Utah in the persons of U.S. associate justice W.W. Drummond and his mistress. Not kidding. The powers that be in Washington, D.C., appointed a gentile adulterer/child deserter to the Utah Territorial Court. Don't think the Mormons didn't make hay with that bureaucratic snafu.

Judge William Wormer Drummond (thanks to the *Deseret News* for digging up W.W.'s awesome middle name) abandoned his wife and five children back in Illinois to take up with Ada Carroll, nicknamed "Skinny Ada," whom he brought with him to Utah. History records Skinny Ada as either a former prostitute or another man's wife, an understandable confusion, since folks back then didn't distinguish between the two. Drummond claimed he was divorced, but that was a lie.

Brigham Young called Drummond "vain as a peacock and ignorant as a jackass." He wasn't wrong. Drummond's judgeship in Utah was short-lived. He returned to Chicago and worked as a sewing machine salesman until 1885, when he was sent to prison for stealing postage stamps. You can't make this stuff up.

In 1869, George Q. Cannon, the brother of Martha Hughes's future husband Angus Cannon, said, "The nations of Christendom are crowded with prostitutes....How shall these fearful evils be cured?...The Lord, through His people—the Latter-day Saints—is revealing the remedy....If [polygamy] were universally adopted, the 'social evil' would be removed and prostitution would soon cease to exist on the face of the Earth." He was overstating his case, considering the first prophet Joseph Smith had forty-plus wives and was still rumored to have visited ladies of negotiable affection, but that bit of trivia was already ancient history in this fast-evolving religion.

Once in Utah under the leadership of the Second Prophet, Mormons worked to keep sex work in check. Their first big challenge came with the 1857 arrival (they called it an "invasion") of the U.S. Army and its attendant camp followers. Then came the passengers on the transcontinental railroad, which first reached Utah in 1869. The railroad brought a market for both sex and alcohol.

"It is a very curious circumstance in this land of freedom, that while there are a great many persons who would willingly accept severe legislation to prohibit plural marriage, there are not a few persons, some of them the very same persons, who are in favor of licensing prostitution," the *Deseret Evening News* opined in 1876.

Dr. Mattie's brother-in-law George Q. Cannon added, "Our crime has been: We married women instead of seducing them, we reared children instead of destroying them, we desired to exclude from the land prostitution, bastardy, and infanticide."

In the long run, the Mormons' prating about hypocrisy did next to nothing to protect them legally, which is not to say that their message didn't have any impact. Even non-Mormons came to equate adultery with polygamy. In 1872, New York writer Elizabeth Tilton confessed her adulterous affair to her husband in these words: "H[enry] W[ard] Beecher, my friend and pastor…solicited me to *be a wife* to him, together with all that this implied" (emphasis added). Mrs. Tilton did not petition for a divorce from Mr. Tilton before accepting Reverend Beecher's solicitation to "be a wife to him," which is how we know that, even to her and her gentile lover, polygamy and adultery were pretty much the same thing.

Likewise, suffragist and feminist Elizabeth Cady Stanton equated polygamy with the well-known form of marriage "involving one wife and many mistresses," which was "everywhere practiced in the United States." James Gibbons, the Roman Catholic archbishop of Baltimore, preached that divorce and remarriage constitute "successive polygamy."

The law saw these things as distinctly different. In 1882, the Mormons argued that the Edmunds Act, which banned polygamists from voting, serving on juries and holding office, should also be enforced against fornicators and adulterers. Nobody took them seriously. As a practical political matter, both political parties would have seen that as a major threat to their voting base. In the twenty-first century, the Adultery Caucus is still the biggest bipartisan

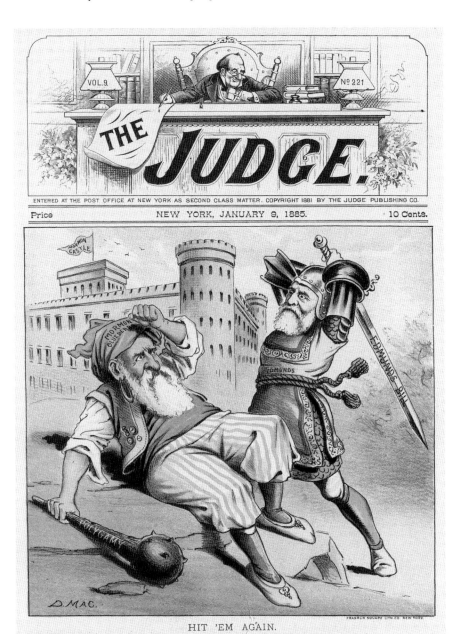

Congress couldn't slay polygamy. *Library of Congress, LC-DIG-ds-14610.*

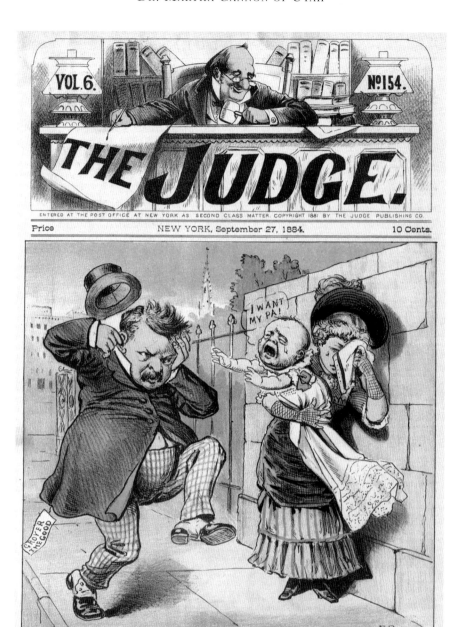

Grover Cleveland's rape scandal didn't keep him out of the White House. *Library of Congress, LC-DIG-ppmsca-15780.*

influence in Washington. (That's a joke. There's no Adultery Caucus, just like there's no bipartisan influence.)

Then and now, the fact that few Americans care about hypocrisy doesn't stop those who do care from tilting at windmills. Just two years after the Edmunds Act was passed to persecute polygamists, Grover Cleveland was elected president. The renowned pastor George Ball described Grover to the press as "a champion libertine, an artful seducer, a foe to virtue…and hostile to true womanhood."

After the election, in a petition addressed to the foe of virtue himself, President Cleveland, the Mormons sought redress from the Edmunds law, inserting some absolutely luscious snark: "The paramour of mistresses and harlots, secure from prosecution, walks the streets in open day. No United States official puts a spotter on his 'trail,' or makes an effort to drag his deeds of guilt and shame before a judge and jury."

Well, that must have stung—or not. At any rate, the paramour in the White House ignored the petition.

ADULTERY AFFECTED MORMONS, TOO—AT least a little bit—in spite of polygamy. Mattie and Angus's nephew John Q. Cannon confessed to adultery in 1886. John Q. and his lover had "decided against" plural marriage. He was excommunicated by Angus himself.

Nevertheless, the pioneer polygamists in Utah did a better job respecting women and supporting children than their peers in the rest of the country. A polygamous wife had an exalted social status no gentile mistress or sex worker could ever hope to attain in her wildest dreams. When a polygamous man tired of his wife, he just took another. Mormon men rarely filed for divorce. While each new wife trimmed the frequency of visits to earlier and older wives, they retained their respectability in the community. None of a polygamist's children were called bastards by their neighbors. Fathers accepted financial responsibility. A good and faithful polygamist's children didn't have to be abandoned to an orphan train or orphanage by destitute mothers.

While polygamists' children weren't bastardized, abandoned or raised without the financial support of their fathers, money only stretches so far. Men can work harder and longer to support more children, but every day is still just twenty-four hours long. Plus, Mormon men were sent abroad for years at a time to be missionaries for the faith, leaving their wives at home to fend for themselves.

The pragmatic Second Prophet Brigham Young saw that he could not build a bustling economy, a prosperous Zion, if half the population stayed shuttered inside, sewing buttons and wiping noses, while their husbands gallivanted across the ocean. That was as plain as the nose on his face, the dome of his tabernacle or the glint off the waters of the Great Salt Lake. Therefore, Zion's women should submit to their husbands, but they should also be educated, well-trained, gainfully employed and well-paid. Women should be artisans, business managers and highly educated professionals— doctors, especially. Brigham Young wanted women physicians for Zion.

8

GET TO WORK, LADIES! BUILD BUSINESSES! BIRTH BABIES!

Mattie Paul Hughes came of age at a time when Brigham Young was on a tear to put Mormon women to work. Other biographers emphasize that Mattie's early childhood experiences, watching the deaths of her baby sister on the Mormon Trail and her father upon her arrival in Salt Lake City, inspired her to study medicine. Among her first memories, these tragedies surely imprinted deeply, but plenty of non-Mormon girls grieved the deaths of loved ones and never dreamed of becoming doctors. The Second Prophet's zeal for women's higher education and gainful employment certainly played a role in teenage Mattie's decision to go to college.

In 1851, before Mattie was born and while her parents still lived in Wales, the University of Deseret's enrollment was almost 50/50 men and women. Among U.S. university students at the time, fewer than 25 percent were women, and this is no wonder. Education would drive you mad, warned the non-Mormon *Ladies' Companion* magazine in 1847. Darkly, ominously, the magazine warned that diverting blood and energy from the womb to the brain turned a woman into a "semi-woman," a "mental hermaphrodite." Egads! A little less frighteningly, the 1873 book *Sex in Education* merely cautioned that the energy a woman spent studying depleted her reproductive capacity.

Daring to turn yourself into an infertile mental hermaphrodite took a lot of courage, indeed. Still, a brave few were willing to risk it. A handful of colleges and universities in the United States admitted women alongside men, the first being Oberlin College in Ohio; plus, there were some women-only colleges. Brain scans had not yet been invented, so we are unable to ascertain how the cells in the women students' brains reorganized themselves hermaphroditically. Nevertheless, the majority of these allegedly infertile university-educated "semi-women" were channeled into the teaching profession.

Brigham Young would have none of that. He refused to corral the women of Zion into one profession. "We wish the sisters, so far as their inclinations and circumstances permit," he said in 1868 (when Mattie was in grade school), "to learn bookkeeping, telegraphy, reporting, typesetting, clerking in stores and banks and every branch of knowledge and kind of employment suitable to their sex and according to their several tastes and capacities." As for the depletion of reproductive capacity? The man charged by God with peopling a new Zion through the practice of polygamy spurned that nonsense, too. "Thus trained, all without distinction of sex, will have an open field, without jostling and oppression, for acquiring *all the knowledge* and doing all the good their physical and *mental capacities* and surrounding circumstances will permit" (emphasis added).

To Brigham, a suitable job wasn't necessarily traditionally female, it just meant the work was not physically strenuous. He thought it absolutely bonkers for healthy men to be sewing collars on jackets while women were out "plowing, raking, and making hay," which women were actually doing. Somebody had to, right?

Young preached that a person should follow his or her God-given talents (especially hers). "The education of females ought to be more thorough and practical than it generally is," he said in 1869.

> *For instance, wherever our school mistresses find a natural turn in their female pupils for the study of mathematics, or any particular branch of learning, a class ought to be formed for the special study of that branch of education. You will find but few females especially who have a natural inclination for the study of mathematics, but where it does exist, such a woman, when properly trained, is just as capable of keeping a set of books and occupying a seat in a counting house as a man; and the labor is not too arduous.*

Don't get too judgy over his assumption that few women are inclined to math. We're *still* debating if boys are better at math than girls. *Scientific American* took up the question in 2018. *Psychology Today* ran an article on it in 2019. WebMD put its opinion on the subject online in 2020. What was remarkable

Mattie earned college tuition typesetting. *iStock.*

then—and would still sound remarkable in certain circles today—is his insistence that a woman so inclined is "just as capable" as a man.

These weren't just words, either. Mormon women really did have more educational and economic freedom than women outside Utah. An 1874 visitor to Utah was startled by all the professional women she met there. "They close no career on a woman in Utah," she reported. The *Woman's Exponent* could not contain its glee when two women were admitted to the Utah bar as practicing lawyers: "[H]ere in Utah, decried, abused and maligned as it has been, women enjoy more of what is contended for as women's rights than they do in any State in the Federal Union."

The Second Prophet's motives were practical. He had a big job to do, and it was all hands on deck. "Let us no longer sit with hands folded, wasting time, for it is the duty of every man and every woman to do all that is possible to promote the kingdom of God on Earth," he said in 1875. "We believe women are useful, not just to sweep houses, wash dishes, make beds, and raise babies, but that they should stand behind the counter, study law or physic....In following these things, they are but answering the design of their creation."

Not only that, but the free market being what it is, any job not getting done by Mormon hands would get filled by a gentile. Brigham Young couldn't keep gentiles out of Utah, but he wanted his people to shop at Mormon stores, take their disputes to Mormon lawyers and show their rashes to Mormon doctors, all while sending Mormon men back east and overseas to wrangle converts.

To make this work, women needed legal emancipation as well. First off, married women had to own real estate in their own names. In most of the rest of the United States in the nineteenth century, married women could not own or purchase real estate or enter into contracts. That was just impractical in polygamous Utah. With men gone overseas for years at a time, the women they left behind had to have authority to take care of their property and businesses. It's not like they could get hubby's signature on a contract by emailing a pdf back and forth.

Inheritance was also tricky. Only the first wife would inherit by law. If a husband wanted his wives to keep their own homes and businesses upon his death, plural wives had to own property outright.

Financially independent wives scared the gee willikers out of non-Mormons at the time. "Men do not like, and would not seek, to mate with an independent factor who at any time could quit the tedious duties of training and bringing up children, and keeping the tradesmen's bills, and mending the linen, for the more lucrative returns of the desk or counter," opined the 1857 non-Mormon *Saturday Review*. Latter-day Saints couldn't afford that kind of worry. Plus, the polygamous wives had an advantage: work sharing.

Pioneer womanhood was exhausting. All that lugging wood for the stove, scrubbing clothes over a washboard and hauling water for the bath. Today's turn-the-knob washers and jetted hot tubs would have been too fantastical for pioneers to even imagine. Gentile women on the frontier had no choice but to plow, prune, pluck, press and potty train, often on their own from dusk to dawn.

Anthropologist Burton put it this way in 1860: "Life in the wilds of Western America is a course of severe toil; a single woman cannot perform the manifold duties of housekeeping, cooking, scrubbing, washing, darning, child-bearing, and nursing a family. A division of labor is necessary, and she finds it by acquiring a sisterhood." In polygamy, each wife could specialize in the duties she enjoyed most or despised least. The craftsy one might take on spinning, weaving and sewing, leaving the gardening, milking and cooking to her culinary sister wife. A third wife could keep the tradesmen's bills while a fourth mended the linen. Never mind the opinion of the *Saturday Review*, many women do not consider childrearing "tedious" at all, and those wives were glad to keep an eye on a few more kids if it got them out of scrubbing clothes on the washboard.

Nineteenth-century Mormon women weren't necessarily rushing outside the home for paid work, at least not relative to the way women work today. In our twenty-first century, 60 percent of married women, gentile and Mormon alike, work outside the home. Back in Mattie Paul Hughes's day, just 12 percent of polygamous wives worked outside the home. But that was *double* the percentage of monogamous women who took jobs in the rest of the United States at the time. Plus, the LDS Church encouraged home-based manufacturing by women. Just because women didn't leave the house, doesn't mean they weren't making money. The first wife of Jacob Voss was an expert weaver who out-earned her husband. His second wife built a thriving butter and egg business. Jacob had a reputation for ineptitude, but he had terrific taste in wives.

Polygamous wife Daisy Yates Barclay said: "I had the attitude of many Mormon women in polygamy. I felt the responsibility of my family, and I developed an independence that women in monogamy never know." Another polygamous wife, Mrs. Pope, said, "Whenever Brother Pope sent us money, we were glad to get it, but we got along by ourselves when we had to."

Long after Mattie Paul Hughes Cannon was polygamously married, only to see polygamy banned, she told Beatrice Webb in England: "If plural marriage had been allowed to continue, practiced freely, it would have given women an independent life." While it lasted, polygamy did profit from women's industry.

Women's silk production was a big success in Zion. Brigham Young offered free mulberry trees to women who wanted to take up the breeding of silkworms, called sericulture. "Let the beauty of your adorning be the work of your own hands," he said. In 1900, the sericulturalist women of Utah sent a bolt of handmade black silk to Susan B. Anthony as a birthday gift. She had a dress made out of it, which was and maybe still is on display at the Susan B. Anthony Museum and House in Rochester, New York.

In the outside world, male tailors sewing suits for men earned significantly more money than female seamstresses sewing dresses for women. Brigham Young could not see the logic in this. "We are told a woman cannot make a coat, vest, or a pair of pantaloons [men's clothing]. Tell me they cannot pull a thread tight enough, and that they cannot press hard enough to press a coat. It is all folly and nonsense."

Silk-making, a profitable female enterprise. *Public domain; L. Tom Perry Special Collections, Harold B. Lee Library, Brigham Young University.*

He was open-minded about other nontraditional careers, too. When asked if women could become sheriffs, Young didn't miss a beat, replying that he thought one of his wives, the six-foot-tall Harriet Cook Young, would make an excellent sheriff. If she "went out after a man, she would get him every time." Whether Harriet wanted to become sheriff was left unexamined.

Women also proved themselves strong enough to press ink onto paper as journalists and more. "A woman can write as well as a man, and spell as well as a man, and better," said Brigham Young. He encouraged "our girls" to become typesetters and telegraph operators. He believed both women and men could have a taste for mechanics, art and science. Young also encouraged women to run cooperative stores. He said he couldn't stand watching "a big, lubberly fellow handing out calicoes and measuring ribbon; I would rather see the ladies do it." He also trusted women to keep accurate financial records.

Young's legacy lived on after his death. The sixth president of the church, Joseph F. Smith (nephew of the church's founder Joseph Smith), said, "The woman who performed the same kind and quality of work that a man did, should receive therefore the same wages of pay. If a woman as school teacher, clerk, accountant or cook excelled a man in those same occupations, she should receive superior pay, and it is a poor rule that did not work both ways."

While Mormon women excelled at business, silk manufacturing and the like, not many took up Brigham Young's invitation to pursue professional careers in law and engineering. Medicine was another matter.

The Latter-day Saints in Zion were enthusiastic to send their daughters back east to study medicine. Given a choice, women preferred female doctors. (Even today, twice as many women prefer female doctors as men who prefer male doctors.) And Mormons preferred Mormon doctors.

Mattie Paul Hughes heard the call. She was eager to go.

9

GO EAST, YOUNG WOMAN!

Mattie Learns Medicine "In the World"

T he time has come for women to come forth as doctors in these valleys and mountains," Brigham Young exhorted his followers in 1873.

The first Mormon woman to answer Brigham Young's call to go east "into the world" to study modern medicine was not Mattie Paul Hughes. It was Romania Bunnell Pratt. In 1873, she enrolled in Bellevue College in New York, leaving her young children at home in Utah under the care of her mother. By the end of her first year of school, she was broke. It didn't help that her husband, Parley, had taken another wife in her absence. He couldn't afford to support one wife at home and pay the tuition for another "abroad." So, Romania went home.

But not so fast! Romania's Mormon friends rallied to her side. They raised enough money to send her back to school, this time to the Woman's Medical College in Philadelphia. In 1877, she brought her newly engraved medical diploma back to Salt Lake City. Dr. Pratt may have been the "reputable female physician" anti-Mormon propagandist Jennie Anderson Froiseth described as having "a very large practice in Salt Lake City." Froiseth clucked her disapproval: "[Mormons] never employ male physicians except in extreme cases" (like that was a bad thing).

Next up was Margaret Shipp, one of Milford Shipp's wives. Margaret dropped out of school almost immediately but encouraged her sister wife Ellis Shipp to go in her stead. Ellis was relieved to get to Philadelphia in 1875. "I am tired of this life of cooking, washing dishes, and general housework....

[A woman] should have ample time and opportunity to improve her mind," Ellis said. Even so, she missed her kids. "My darling sweet children," she wrote to them, "how Mama longs to see you. Oh, how my heart aches." It's unclear how many children Ellis left behind in Utah to go to medical school. Some sources say three, and others say five. What we do know for sure is that she gave birth to another child while in Pennsylvania. And if you think she took a break or dropped out, you'd be wrong.

Ellis soldiered on. Per the *Woman's Exponent*:

> *She passed through, with proud and faithful resignation, the hopeful, anxious time of motherhood, giving birth, while still at college, to a beautiful child, on the twenty-fifth of May, 1877. As soon as her attendants allowed, she was again engaged in her studies, with her new little new born babe constantly near, that she might care for her, herself….Mrs. Shipp obtained as high a degree in as short a period as others who had no children near to engage their time and attention.*

Dr. Mrs. Shipp brought home her baby and her degree in 1878. She must have been quite the inspiration. Her sister wife Margaret, the one who had previously dropped out, returned to school and earned her own medical degree in 1883.

GETTING AN MD WAS quite a bit simpler for Mattie Paul Hughes. She was unmarried and childless when she answered the call. Working through college was still a viable financial strategy in the nineteenth century, and that's what Mattie did. At the age of fifteen, she had taken up Brigham Young's invitation to learn typesetting, which she did for the *Deseret News*. Later, she set type for the *Woman's Exponent*, where she met the matriarchs of Mormonism, Eliza Snow and Emmeline Wells. At nineteen, she enrolled in the University of Deseret, majoring in chemistry. Two years later, in 1878, Mattie Paul Hughes graduated from the University of Deseret and was accepted into the University of Michigan Medical School.

The University of Michigan allowed women to study in any department they wished, which was so unusual that Elizabeth Mosher (class of 1875) and her friends "joined hands and danced around the table." At the age of twenty-one, Mattie left Utah with the blessing of her family, her church and her mentors Eliza Snow and Emmeline Wells. Her stepfather, James Paul, loaned her $10 a month to cover her living expenses. (That's about $300 after a century and a half of inflation.) Eliza gave Mattie a $20 gold piece in a purse she knitted herself.

Even with that big-hearted financial support, Mattie had to work to support herself in Michigan. She cleaned the dormitory, washed dishes and took work as a secretary. She wasted no time on trivialities. To save time in the morning, she cut her hair short, like she'd worn it as a child. This was a radical act in an age when adult women never cut their hair and spent hours a day twisting and pinning their long tresses into fancy knots and upsweeps.

Mattie became Dr. Mattie P. Hughes when she was awarded a medical degree on her twenty-third birthday in 1880. She began practicing medicine in Michigan in

Mattie's short curls saved time. *By permission, Utah State Historical Society.*

1881. Her audacity made headlines immediately. A woman does an operation! Very skillfully, no less! The *Marine City Reporter* ate it up. Dr. Mattie's former employers at the *Woman's Exponent* couldn't wait to reprint the details with their usual glowing admiration for "a girl well known and highly esteemed in Utah." They reprinted the details from *Marine City Reporter*:

> *A very skillful surgical operation pertaining to vesico-vaginal fistula was performed in Algonac on Wednesday, by Miss Mattie P. Hughes, M.D., with the assistance of Drs. Moore, of Algonac, and W.H. Smith, of St. Clair. Dr. Slocum had been invited to take part in the operation, but declined to play "second fiddle" to a woman….*[Dr. Slocum] *felt they were compromising their dignity by assisting a lady in a very difficult operation upon one of her own sex.*

The *Marine City Reporter* took Dr. Mattie's side in the dispute, praising her superior scholarship, courage, self-reliance and, perhaps most importantly of all, her "obliging disposition and lady like deportment."

By the time Mattie performed this headline-making surgery, she had already been accepted for further studies at the University of Pennsylvania. "Miss Hughes, the Salt Lake girl, has entered [the University of Pennsylvania] with 100 gentlemen, the only lady in the class," the *Woman's*

Exponent exclaimed in 1881. "We rejoice in her prosperity, and sincerely hope she may attain the highest excellence possible in the profession."

In Pennsylvania, Mattie studied medical jurisprudence, toxicology, forensic medicine, hygiene and botany. She wrote her thesis on "mountain fever," that scourge of the Mormon Trail. She also earned a degree, with honors, from the National School of Elocution and Oratory, perhaps because she wanted to learn how to effectively communicate healthy practices to her patients. Maybe she looked to become an effective voice for women's suffrage. Or maybe (just maybe) she had an eye toward someday running for elected office.

In 1882, Dr. Mattie returned home to her mother and stepfather in their "little cottage under the hill [in] my dear old Rocky Mountains." She set up a clinic in their home, bought a horse and buggy for house calls and got herself hired at Deseret Hospital. It was at the hospital where she was destined to meet the much older but exceedingly charming hospital board member and esteemed Mormon church leader and polygamist Angus Cannon.

Mark Twain satirized Mormons (and everyone else). *Library of Congress, LC-DIG-ppmsca-55329.*

MATTIE'S DEAR OLD ROCKY Mountains were then and still are a remarkably healthy place. In 2018, *People* magazine decided Salt Lake City was the healthiest city in the United States. Way back in 1872, Mark Twain joked about the same thing: "Salt Lake City was healthy— an extremely healthy city. They declared there was only one physician in the place and he was arrested every week regularly and held to answer under the vagrant act for having 'no visible means of support.'"

Oh, but the babies and all those wives! In a polygamous society that was not immune from the influence of the Cult of True Womanhood, women doctors were valued as midwives and for treating female patients who were too embarrassed to show their lady bits to male doctors.

However, the Second Prophet's plea for women physicians was to ensure there were enough Mormon doctors to treat Mormon patients—both men and women. As Eliza

Snow put it, "We want sister physicians who can officiate in any capacity… and unless they educate themselves the [gentile] gentlemen that are flocking in our midst will do it."

Drs. Pratt, Shipp, Cannon and the second Shipp were not limited to treating women. We know Mattie did not limit herself. She handled all manner of Mormon maladies, including "a case of the most intricate and complicated hip-joint disease." We know a certain John Wooley went to Dr. Romania Pratt when he got a barleycorn stuck in his ear. Most remarkable was Angus Cannon, who took his "piles" (that is, hemorrhoids) to that same Dr. Pratt. If you think the lady doc let the anally afflicted president of the Salt Lake Stake of the Latter-day Saints keep his trousers on, think again: "I underwent a most rigid examination at the hands of one I have confidence in," he reported afterward.

Eventually, male physicians began pushing back against the women, even in obstetrics and gynecology. The *Woman's Exponent* pulled no punches in defending the pioneer women physicians. In 1894, the newspaper opined:

> *There is no wonder that there is such a cry against women as physicians in Utah. The men know if this department of medicine was occupied by women, many of them would have to turn to other pursuits or seek other climes of livelihood, which would no doubt be a good thing for Utah. For while we realize that we have many men who are fine physicians and gentlemen, we have many whose characters would not bear inspection and are not fit creatures to wait on the fair daughters of Zion….I am not afraid to say that the mortality in the same number of cases and conditions is not nearly so great with our women physicians as with men physicians.*

A year later, self-described "True Woman" J.P.M. Farnsworth complained about the prejudice of medical schools against women students and concluded:

> *We wish our doctors (our lady doctors) every success. We desire them to be highly educated in all branches of scientific study, to improve every opportunity to grasp every advanced idea that presents itself, to keep pace with the glorious age we live in, to be thorough, accurate, systematic and capable; to have dignity and gentleness combined, modesty, purity, neatness, order and love pervade their every walk in life and thereby, prove that they are just what we would wish them to be, ministering angels on earth.*

Amen, sister.

WOMEN DOCTORS WERE POPULAR outside of Utah, too. In the 1800s, the top two (legal) professions for women were teaching and medicine. By the end of the era, 10 percent of U.S. physicians were women, a percentage that might not seem impressive now but was enough to ignite a gigantic backlash. Forty years into the twentieth century, the number of women doctors had plummeted to a measly 4 percent. Women physicians wouldn't get back to their 1900 peak until the middle of the 1970s.

What was it that attracted those delicate and domesticated, coy and corseted Victorian women to medicine? The gentile ladies were not answering a plea from the Second Prophet, that's for sure. Why, it was the Cult of True Womanhood! What else? And you thought we were done with that subject? No such luck.

Accouchement, which means childbirth (nothing obviated Victorian scruples better than a nifty euphemism, preferably French), was the largest and most obvious conundrum, even for monogamists. Midwives had fallen out of fashion, but it was mortifying for a True Woman to show her lady bits to a grubby man, never mind his fancy diploma! The rise in deaths from puerperal fever was another concern. It couldn't be that those university-educated male doctors didn't know what they were doing! It couldn't be that they never bothered to wash their hands, a notion that didn't even occur to the earliest Victorians. There was only one possible explanation: puerperal convulsions were caused by "female delicacy, grievously shocked by the presence and personal attention of a gentleman."

In addition to childbirth, women had all these other inscrutable and peculiar health problems. Female bodies contained this cosmic reproductive mystery. The speculum was invented to give doctors a view into a woman's enigmatic recesses, but yikes! The immodesty! In 1856, a newspaper column titled "Hints to Husbands" warned against letting wives be examined by male doctors: the "most inmost secrets of your wife's person are known to him, the veil of modesty has been rudely torn aside." A British doctor blamed prostitution on the dual temptations of "Indian hemp" (or pot, also known as marijuana or cannabis) and the speculum. Women readers, answer this: upon "enjoying" the chill steel of a speculum, don't you feel like smoking cannabis and charging for your sexual services? No? Or maybe just yes to the weed part?

What were the Victorians to do? It was a vexation. One Samuel Gregory had the answer. He was the nineteenth century's loudest and proudest campaigner for women's medical education. Make no mistake, Dr. Gregory was not so progressive as the Mormons. He would not have dreamed of

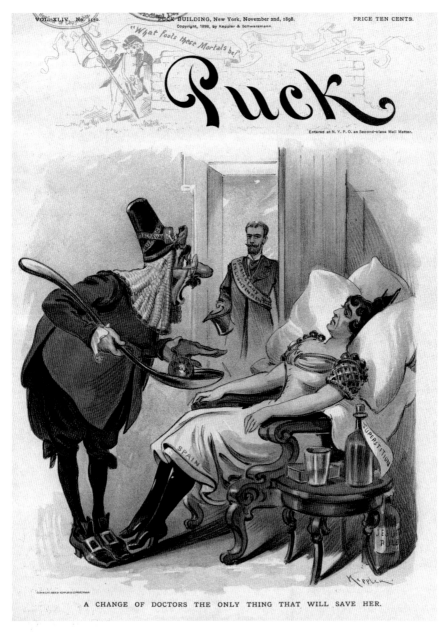

Modesty recommended women docs for women patients. *Library of Congress, LC-DIG-ppmsca-28643.*

encouraging a woman to examine the burning bottom of a respectable man like Dr. Romania Pratt did for Angus Cannon. Samuel Gregory's crusade was to recruit women to be doctors for women and children. It was more proper, not to mention that attending to childbirth was beneath the dignity of a man and a waste of his valuable time. Goodness gracious, birthing a baby could take hours!

It just made sense that half of doctors should be women. "There are said to be forty thousand physicians in the United States," Gregory wrote in an 1856 fundraising appeal for his proposed Boston Female Medical College. "Twenty-thousand of those ought to give place to this number of women, and turn their attention to pursuits better adapted to their strong muscles and strong minds than is this waiting with ladies from two to twenty hours, and this simple, mechanical routinism of midwifery."

Gregory was also concerned for women who avoided treatment for other maladies particular to their sex. "So great, indeed, is the embarrassment arising from fastidiousness on the part of the female herself, or of the [male] practitioner, or both, that I am persuaded that much of the ill success of treatment may be justly tied thereto." It wasn't enough to train nurses to assist male physicians; women must be in charge, he said.

Gregory had a ready answer for every objection to women practicing medicine. To those who said it was just not done, he pointed to the women midwives who were common sights in colonial America and were still common in Europe and on southern plantations. In the South, it was common for an enslaver to call upon one of his enslaved women to midwife his wife's babies. To those who claimed that women would not venture out at night or in bad weather, Gregory responded: "True women…rarely quail when duty and humanity call them to face danger.…There will be ways for doctoresses to get about."

Progressive women got on the bandwagon. Susan B. Anthony said, "Whoever controls work and wages controls morals. Therefore, we must have woman employers, superintendents, legislators…preachers, lawyers, doctors, that wherever women go to seek counsel—spiritual, legal, physical—there, too, they will be sure to find the best and noblest of their own sex to minister to them."

Dr. Mattie Paul Hughes Cannon would eventually answer two of Anthony's calls—as a doctor and legislator.

THE BRUTAL BACKLASH AGAINST women doctors came in the twentieth century. Female medical schools closed as women preferred the greater scientific rigor of coeducational universities. At the same time, the guys didn't like being shown up by women, so coeducational schools began limiting women to make up no more than 5 percent of the student body. In 1890, women counted for 25 percent of the students at Dr. Mattie's alma mater, the University of Michigan Medical School. By 1910, women made up only 3 percent of the student body. (Quotas were lifted temporarily only in response to dire national emergencies, such as World War I and World War II. This is what's known as the exceptions that prove the rule.)

Another factor was the fast fading of the Cult of True Womanhood. Cigarette-smoking, bead-twirling, short-skirted flappers were dancing on the horizon. Educating women to care for women took the rumble seat to the more fashionable issues of the early twentieth century—women's suffrage, liquor prohibition and comfier clothing. Once the flappers started boogeying the Charleston, the Cult of True Womanhood was history.

It was not until the 1970s that the number of women doctors rebounded to the 10 percent peak of 1900. It wasn't until 2017 that we finally reached Samuel Gregory's 1856 dream of gender parity in medical training. Interestingly, though, today's women medical residents primarily specialize in the exact fields Samuel Gregory recommended—OB/GYN and pediatrics (plus family medicine and psychiatry). And here's the weirdest twenty-first-century twist: the percentage of male OB/GYNs has fallen so low that the medical establishment is considering lowering its standards to attract more men to the field.

On that odd note, we return to the story of the indomitable Mattie Paul Hughes, who left graduate studies to return home to Utah, with a boyfriend in tow.

10

FIRST COMES LOVE, THEN COMES MARRIAGE, THEN COMES BABY

Our fistula-fixing Mattie Paul Hughes was in no hurry to get married when she returned to Utah from graduate school. She brought along with her a young man, newly converted to Mormonism, who had fallen for the slim, fresh-faced young woman with a coy smile, kind eyes of hazel hue and short, curly brown hair.

Her first task was to recover from meningitis. Mattie's parents let the besotted young man live in their home to help care for her. Whatever his nursing skills and other charms may have been, the courtship fell short. This was not the first time this happened to Mattie. She had abandoned a serious beau four years earlier to study medicine and broke a few more hearts along the way. Nobody measured up.

Once she recovered from brain fever, as meningitis was then known, the twenty-five-year-old ignored her doctor's fuddy-duddy prescription to avoid "brain work" and set to building her medical practice. The brand-spanking-new Deseret Hospital (whose cost of care was $6 per day, or $150 today) invited the young doctor to join its staff. One day, so the story goes, Dr. Mattie was busy at work when a certain board trustee entered the room to do whatever it was that board trustees feel it is important to do. Mattie looked at this round-headed, mustachioed trustee who was old enough to be her father and told him to get out. She had work to do. Her cheekiness charmed Angus Cannon. He left the room but not her life.

Forty-eight-year-old Angus Cannon was dashingly handsome, charismatic and known for his tidy grooming and scrupulous cleanliness. He typically

Angus Cannon. *By permission, Utah State Historical Society.*

sported a silk top hat and snazzy double-breasted Prince Albert frock coat, which featured a flat velvet collar, three large buttons down the front and a shaped waistline. That Victorian symbol of male gentility, the silver-handled walking stick, completed his ensemble.

Angus had a Renaissance man's resume. He had been a farmer, rancher, printer's apprentice, business manager, missionary and potter. He had been elected the mayor of St. George, Utah, and the president of the Salt Lake Stake of the Church of Jesus Christ of Latter-day Saints. (A stake is a division of the LDS Church composed of several wards, or congregations.)

By the time Dr. Mattie shooed him out of the room, Angus Cannon had three wives and seventeen children, but his primary devotion was the church. He would never rise to the height achieved by his more famous brother

George Q., a member of the Quorum of Twelve Apostles, but Angus's position as president of the Salt Lake Stake was nothing to shake a stick at (not even a silver walking stick).

In Dr. Mattie, he met his match. Their courtship was tricky, polygamy being federally illegal. At one point, Mattie and Angus went on an overnight buggy trip together, the usually nattily tailored Angus cleverly disguised in a blue shirt, red neckerchief and farmer's overalls. They stopped for the night at the home of Mrs. Elizabeth Owen. "I offered Mr. Cannon and the lady the bed to sleep together, but he said they were not married," she testified later in court. "I then offered her the bed and she said the lounge would do." Mrs. Owen further testified she was pretty sure "the lady" was Dr. Mattie, since she gave Elizabeth a short course in pharmacology, listing the ingredients of the patent medicines she saw on the home's medicine shelf, including the morphine.

Mattie became Angus's fourth wife on October 6, 1884, sealed "for time and eternity" at a secret ceremony at the Endowment House in Salt Lake City. The federal officials were cracking down hard on polygamists. Supposedly, Mattie did not tell her mother about the marriage and continued lying to her friends. Or maybe she told them and vowed them to secrecy. We can't know for sure what Mattie's mother knew about the marriage, but we do know she told a court, under oath, that she hadn't a clue the two were married. (Or so she testified. Perjury was not out of the question. Lying for the Lord was a pretty well-practiced thing for the early Mormons.) Mattie described her honeymoon year as "a few stolen interviews thoroughly tinctured with the dread of discovery."

Why would a pretty, intelligent, educated and talented young woman agree to become illegal secret wife number four? As a university-educated, trained physician, Dr. Mattie would have almost certainly out-earned any young husband. Mormons may have been progressive about women's rights, but even so, a monogamous wife of a man just starting out would have felt pressure to give up her career. Angus, on the other hand, had long ago proven his financial wherewithal and, considering that he was supporting three other wives and seventeen children, appreciated the financial independence of wife number four.

But what about love? We wonder, just as her friends did at the time. When her marriage was no longer secret, Mattie described Angus in a letter to her gentile friend Barbara Replogle. Angus, she wrote, was "all but perfection in my eyes." Mattie wrote to Angus that he was "the only man that I have ever loved," and "I would rather spend one hour in your society than a whole life time with any other man I know of." Also, "just accept a bushel of kisses and remember that I think heaps of you."

The feeling was mutual. Angus wrote: "You have been loved as much as any woman has been, are, and yet will be loved, as only a true heart is capable of loving."

Their age difference did not go unnoticed. Mattie's pet names for Angus were "My Old Duck," "Old Sweetheart" and "Old Boy." My Old Duck didn't like it. "I should not like you to call me by such endearing names," he quacked or, rather, complained. "The facts are it [is] too near the truth which is not always relished by the best of us." Mattie was, after all, two years younger than Angus's oldest son.

Soon, the "few stolen interviews" of Old Sweetheart and the young doctor led to the inevitable. Mattie was pregnant. This was a pickle of prodigious proportions. Federal officials were hunting polygamists. Not only was Dr. Mattie literally carrying incontrovertible evidence of Angus's illegal "cohabitation" and polygamy, but she had also attended the births of many polygamously conceived babies. To protect Angus and her patients, Dr. Mattie fled Utah, baby Elizabeth in her arms.

More on that to come.

A REAL SCOURGE FURTHER confounded the gentiles: surplus women! Victorians fussed and fretted over the problem of women who could not find husbands. They sincerely wished happily-ever-after matrimony for everybody. But when the rule is one man and one woman, you need equal numbers, or there will be leftovers. In the 1800s, the leftovers were women, at least "back east."

In the United States, first the 1848 California gold rush and then the 1858 Colorado gold rush lured men west. Then the Civil War killed more men. Following the secession of the southern states, in the middle of the war, President Lincoln signed the 1862 Homestead Act, which lured more men west. The act offered 160 acres to any citizen who hadn't taken up arms against the Union. Women were eligible to receive land, but not many were eager to break sod all by themselves. In 1865, a few months after the shooting stopped, Horace Greeley of the *New York Daily Tribune* exhorted vets to "Go West, Young Man." (At least, that's how we remember it. What Horace actually wrote in his July 13, 1865 edition was much less catchy: "We earnestly urge upon all such to turn their faces Westward and colonize the public lands.") Single men and families heeded the call. But single women?

Not so much. Unless, of course, they were the kind of women who had a certain kind of business to transact.

Lopsided demographics were deliberated at length in Washington, D.C. According to the March 18, 1868 *Deseret Evening News*:

> *It was claimed in the address* [to the House Committee on Territories] *that the unequal distribution of the sexes in the nation, with its attendant low wages and lives of ill-fame, would be much lessened by enfranchising the women of the Territories. Give them the right of suffrage in the Territories, and they would have greater security in person and property than exists elsewhere, and this, it was argued, would induce the emigration for women from the overcrowded east.*

That strategy was already working in Utah. Women Latter-day Saints, those of marrying age in particular, outnumbered men, but there was

Heber C. Kimball. *Getty Museum.*

absolutely no surplus of women. Indeed, Zion was eagerly importing even more women from abroad. England and Wales gave up more single women to the Mormon missionaries than single men. "Many converts are attracted by the prospect of becoming wives," wrote our good anthropologist Sir Richard F. Burton after visiting Utah. "The old maid is, as she ought to be, an unknown entity [in Utah]."

There were enough polygamists to snatch up every "old maid," divorcée and widow. (In 1864, Mormon Heber Kimball was quoted in the *Atlantic*, thanking the Lord Almighty for providing Civil War widows to Utah polygamists.) Whatever your romantic lot may have been back east, in Utah, there was a husband and a house for you.

11

ONE FEATHER IN THE BIRD

Mormon Polygamy Evolves, Splinters, Molts

Modern LDS members, the black-trousered and white-shirted Mormons satirized in Trey Parker and Matt Stone's *The Book of Mormon* and the ones who control the temple Brigham Young built in Salt Lake City, abandoned plural marriage around the turn of the twentieth century, more or less.

Once Joseph Smith died, Brigham Young could have tried to keep the principle secret and let the practice die out with himself and the handful of others who had followed Smith's lead. Instead, he shared the secret with the rank and file in 1846 at Sugar Creek, Iowa, on their trek to find a promised land safe from gentile mobs. Once the shock had worn off, Mormons embraced plural marriage with all the vim and vigor their pioneer spirits could rustle up. In 1851, Brigham Young told the territorial legislature he was not ashamed of his "many" wives. Salt Lake City mayor Jedediah Grant told Pennsylvania journalist Thomas Kane the practice was necessary because women outnumbered men. It solved the dreadful "surplus women" predicament! In August 1852 came the big reveal. Polygamy was practiced in Utah within full view of the United States and the Victorian world for thirty-eight years. Then they gave it up. What was this all about, anyway?

No instruction manual told Brigham Young how to build a new kingdom of God in the heretofore godforsaken desert of Utah, much less how to introduce polygamy to a bunch of Victorian prudes. But he did it!

In 1852, when the principle of polygamy went public, there was no federal law prohibiting it, only traditional objections. Orson Pratt delivered the public defense at Brigham Young's behest. To paraphrase: It's the grand design of God! It's history! It's in the Bible! Monogamy leads to iniquity! And, last but not least: it will be regulated! Joseph Smith's "wedding" in the haymow with the witness peering through the crack in the door was not at all "regulated."

Times had changed.

A lot of converts unconverted but not everyone. "It caused quite a commotion in our branch," remembered Priscilla Merriman Evans. "There was one girl there who came to me with tears in her eyes and said, 'Is it true that Brigham Young has ninety wives? Oh, I can't stand that!'…I told her I did not see anything to cry about. So after I encouraged her she dried her tears and when we were ready to emigrate she came with us."

Only 10 to 20 percent of Victorian-era Mormon men actually wed more than one wife, and most of those who did had only two wives. A man who wanted plural wives was *supposed to* get his first wife to agree, something Joseph Smith never accomplished. (Emma Smith relented but never consented.) Our anthropologist Ruffian Dick Burton noted, however, that "the consent of the first wife is seldom refused." Angus Cannon's first wife, Sarah, testified that he didn't ask her permission, at least not seriously. She described: "It is a subject that is jested upon considerably." Some guys married on the sly. Plus, there was pressure.

In 1873, Brigham Young threatened monogamous men and their wives, telling them that "in the resurrection," a sole wife would be taken from her husband and given to a polygamist. In 1884, Young's successor, President Taylor, asked all monogamous ward bishops and stake presidents to find a second wife or resign.

While a husband was supposed to get his first wife's consent or, even better, all his wives' consent to marry again, a stubborn wife's refusal could be vetoed. But in some cases, first wives actually sought out new wives for their husbands. (Certain modern fundamentalists still hew to this tradition. In TLC's documentary *Sister Wives*, the wives joke that their husband's first wife, Meri, is head of "mergers and acquisitions.")

Patriarchy prevailed in Utah (there is no question about that), just as it did everywhere in the United States, Europe and virtually all the world at that time. But since populating a new kingdom of God in the Utah desert as quickly as possible was the goal of Mormons, a wife for every man and several wives for some was an effective tactic.

Some of Brigham's wives. *Library of Congress, LC-USZ62-117487.*

To attract multiple wives, Mormons had to offer a lot more than roses and romance. In 1875, Lester Ward of the Smithsonian wrote, "In Utah… that heroic attachment that welds one soul to another for life…is swept down like a gossamer by the poisonous breath of polygamy." (Lester wasn't exactly an unbiased journalist, but he was pretty proficient in the Victorian proclivity for poetic prose.) What the Mormons offered women was freedom and power unprecedented outside of Utah. Women in Zion were guaranteed marriage, with its attendant social respectability, financial stability, a means to space the birth of babies, a built-in support system, economic rights, child care, easy divorce and the vote.

BUXOM, TINY-WAISTED YOUNG WOMEN with pert noses and clear skin (what Victorians called a "bit o' raspberry") have never had much trouble achieving an "advantageous match" then or now, here or there. Victorians were obsessed with the "well-developed bosom" ("heaving breasts," "voluptuous fullness" and "swelling charms"). Some things don't change.

What of flat-chested women? Pudgy-waisted women? Women with bulbous noses or acne scars? What about older women? The weeping widows and disreputable divorcées? Who's going to marry them? Being insufficiently endowed or "over the hill" has always been a disadvantage in the marriage market. In the buyer's market of surplus women, it spelled doom—but not for Mormons. "Some single women of from thirty to forty, whom one might suppose to be embroiderers, or straw bonnet-makers, were obviously going out in quest of husbands," wrote British novelist Charles Dickens in his genteel but cutting description of women emigrants.

The American Mark Twain was less gracious. He said of polygamous wives, "First you'll marry a combination of calico and consumption that's thin as a rail, and next you'll get a creature that's nothing more than dropsy in disguise."

Anthropologist Burton was surprised by the "broken-down and decrepit crones" he saw in Utah, marveling at the big-heartedness Mormons showed in bringing them to Zion.

Humorist Charles Farrar Browne, also known as Artemus Ward, joked that the women he saw in the Salt Lake Temple "will never be slain in cold blood for their beauty."

These men's judgments tell us more about them than the women they described. It's impossible that Mormon women were as ugly as all that. Mattie Hughes was cute! Emmeline Wells had big, beautiful eyes and a rosebud mouth. Ida Smoot Dusenberry was gorgeous. Don't believe me? Google their images. These male gentile fusspots were cruel and callous, pitiless and persnickety and just plain mean. Be as judgmental toward them as they were toward the women of Utah. They deserve it, the wretched bastards.

This isn't to say they didn't make a point or weren't funny. Twain joked, "The man who marries one of them has done an act of Christian charity…and the man that marries sixty of them has done a deed of open-handed generosity." Not all guys were as malicious as Twain and Ward. Regardless, polygamists who were looking to be exalted in the afterlife had a lot to gain by being less picky, and yes, sometimes Mormon polygamy was an act of charity.

"The men thought it a moral duty to see that every woman was married," Brigham Young's jack Mormon grandson Kimball Young, the University of Chicago– and Stanford-educated, PhD-holding sociologist, wrote in 1954. "When they had two or three wives it did not matter much if they took a spinster or a blind girl or an unattractive one as an additional wife."

Comic Artemus Ward lampooned Mormon wives. *Boston Public Library, via the Digital Public Library of America.*

Both the First and Second Prophets married older women and widows, and these women didn't have to be fertile, either. Schoolteacher Eliza Snow was thirty-eight years old when she married Joseph Smith. Brigham Young married her after Smith died, when she was forty years old. Eliza never bore children but is nevertheless venerated to this day as a "mother in Zion."

Clara Mason, Angus Cannon's third wife, was a widow with four children when they were married in 1875. She was thirty-six at the time. They had one daughter together. The historical record is full of other examples of widows who married polygamists. Mary Ann Fielding was forty-four years old when she married Joseph Fielding, whose first wife was just twenty-three at the time. Victorian cougar Rebecca Zeeman married Wilhelm, twenty years her junior, and had a child with him. Lorin C. Woolley married four women, including two "spinster" cousins and a forty-eight-year-old widow.

Also, some widows came as package deals with their daughters. You can't make this stuff up.

It really did happen sometimes, and that became a punchline for gentile jokers. The following is a regular knee-slappin' skit from America's first stand-up comedian, Artemus Ward:

> *I had a man pointed out to me who married an entire family. He had originally intended to marry Jane, but Jane did not want to leave her widowed mother. The other three sisters were not in the matrimonial market for the same reason; so this gallant man married the whole crowd, including the girls' grandmother who had lost all her teeth, and had to be fed with a spoon. The family were in indigent circumstances, and they could not but congratulate themselves on securing a wealthy husband. It seemed to affect the grandmother deeply, for the first words she said on reaching her new home were, "Now, thank God, I shall have gruel reg'lar!"*

Artemus wouldn't make it on Netflix, but President Abraham Lincoln thought he was a hoot.

Occasionally, a man would marry his dead brother's widow. That is known as a levirate marriage, commanded by God in Deuteronomy 25:5; although, for Mormons, it was optional. Levirate marriage is practiced by some of today's fundamentalist Mormons. In the 2017 *Three Wives* documentary, the husband, Jim, married both of his deceased brother's two wives and supported his seven nieces and nephews.

Even divorcées, though stigmatized in the greater nineteenth-century world, could easily find husbands in Utah. John Woolley married the fifty-nine-year-old, twice-divorced, once-widowed Ann Reed Everington in 1886. Marrying divorced women as second and third wives wasn't at all unusual. A divorced and remarried woman in Zion could hold her head up. In the gentile world, divorced women were shamed, considered a "racy breed" and compared to germs that spread disease.

CHILD BRIDES, OR WHAT we consider child brides, were of course a hotter commodity than widows and divorcées. Even when the whole deal was a big secret, first prophet Joseph Smith didn't set age limits. He married some older widows, but he also married teenagers Helen Mar Kimball and Lucy Walker. Right after his successor's 1852 public announcement, there was apparently quite a run on fourteen-year-old girls in Utah. In 1860, the average age of Mormon brides was sixteen; the average age of brides in the rest of the United States was twenty.

The age of people entering their first marriage was rising during the era, so these teenager weddings creeped out a lot of people, gentile and Mormon alike. Sarah Pratt, the first wife of Orson, didn't hold her tongue when her fifty-seven-year-old husband married his tenth wife, sixteen-year-old Margaret Graham: "Here was my husband, gray headed, taking to his bed young girls in mockery of marriage. Of course there could be no joy for him in such an intercourse except the indulgence of his fanaticism and of something else, perhaps, which I hesitate to mention."

While the age of people entering their first marriage rose steadily during the nineteenth century, the trend was complicated by recent history, leftover statutes and economic disparity. Until the last quarter of the nineteenth century, the age of consent by law was ten to twelve years old in most states, except Delaware, where it was just seven. Age of consent laws were not enforced against men who *married* girls, and state laws codified the idea that teenage pregnancy was best solved with shotgun weddings.

The Mormons may have indulged in fanaticism, but their teenage brides were not unique.

To be fair, Mormon enthusiasm for marrying young was not limited to girls. Teenage boys were also encouraged to get hitched. Brigham Young was reported to have said, "Make haste and get married. Let me see *no more boys above sixteen* and girls above fourteen unmarried" (emphasis added), In some of today's fundamentalist polygamous sects (most notoriously, the FLDS of the imprisoned-for-life Warren Jeffs), teenage boys are run off and excommunicated to keep them from competing against the old men. These are the so-called lost boys. That wasn't how it was supposed to work in the old days, although there was a financial reality to contend with. In the 1800s, a sixteen-year-old boy was expected to carry a man's workload, which didn't mean he was paid a man's salary. It was usually easier for a fifty-year-old man to support three wives than it was for a sixteen-year-old to support one.

Angus Cannon, Dr. Mattie's husband, wasn't one of the gray-haired guys panting after nubile teenagers, although he wasn't signing up for Silver Singles, either. Dr. Mattie was twenty-seven when she married Cannon. He was fifty. Wife number five, Maria Bennion, famous for being able to wrestle a calf to the ground, was twenty-nine at her wedding. Wife number six, Joanna Danielson, was thirty-eight. Mattie, Maria and Joanna were all old enough to be considered spinsters, even in the gentile world.

A LOT OF TIMES, Mormon women proposed to the men. Couples were supposed to get the church's permission, but Brigham Young was way too busy to be a one-man OKCupid.com. He did not choose brides for men like prophets do in today's creepier sects, like the ones profiled in *Leaving Bountiful* and *Keep Sweet: Pray and Obey*. Asking for the church's permission seems unnecessarily intrusive, but in the gentile world, men were still asking their beloved's father for her hand in marriage. And this was real, not just a sweet old tradition. Outside of Zion, the prospective bride's father, considered the owner of the "property" that was to be transferred at the wedding, could say no and sometimes did.

Financial considerations were one of the LDS Church's main concerns when approving polygamous matches. Later in life, Dr. Mattie told the *San Francisco Examiner*: "[Mormons] never did let a man marry till he showed conclusively that he could take care of his wife and family. We never raise paupers." Dr. Mattie wasn't exactly lying, but she was definitely stretching the truth. She had to nag Angus to pay his fair share of her rent and money for their children's clothes and "washing powder," even though her independent income was insurance against abject pauperism. And the famed church leader Orson Pratt got permission to marry ten women, even though all his families struggled in poverty. Pratt's church status definitely came into play when he sought permissions to marry.

With the agreement of the woman, finances squared away and the stamp of approval from a church underling, the bride and groom could be "sealed" at the Endowment House. Sealings were supposed to be done in a temple, which is the rule these days, but the Salt Lake City Temple wasn't consecrated until 1893, so the Mormons made do in the meantime.

A very quick primer on Mormon marriage: there are two types of Mormon marriages, "for eternity" (called sealings) and "for time," which are like regular "till death do us part" gentile weddings. Today, LDS temple weddings are "for time and all eternity," and polygamy gets you excommunicated from the mainstream LDS Church. If you're a fundamentalist, you don't care.

PLUCK "ONE FEATHER OF the bird" (in other words, give up polygamy), and the entire Mormon religion would collapse, Apostle Wilford Woodruff warned in 1869. He proved himself wrong. In 1890, the very same Woodruff, having risen from mere apostle to the seat of president of the Quorum of Twelve Apostles, issued a manifesto forbidding future polygamous marriages. The religion survived—thrived even. Like molting, the religion shed the old feather of polygamy to make way for new growth.

Not everybody gave up on polygamy, though. Over one hundred years later, Mormon plural marriage survives in fundamentalist splinter sects in Utah, Arizona, Texas, Missouri and many other places—some really cool places that are usually isolated. The community built into the red ridge at Rockland Ranch in Utah is like a sexy Mesa Verde but with electricity and internet. And like every true red-white-and-blue-blooded American, polygamous Mormons want to be on TV.

TV PRODUCERS LOVE POLYGAMY. It's both educational and erotic, anthropological and erogenous. If you want to watch how twenty-first-century polygamous Mormons live, there are plenty of shows to stream, both documentaries and dramas.

Search your streaming device, and you'll find very conflicting stories. Do today's plural wives wear pastel prairie dresses or ripped skinny jeans? That depends on the sect. Do women choose their husbands, or does their prophet pick for them? Depends on the sect. Are polygamous husbands successful professionals or welfare cheats? Depends on the sect. Do women work "in the world" or stay ensconced at home? Depends on the sect. Do girls marry in their teens or wait until adulthood? Again, that depends on the sect.

There was no one way to live the principle back in the days of Dr. Mattie Hughes and her husband Angus Cannon, but the practice was more homogenous than it is now. Although there's no fundamentalist sect today that exactly replicates nineteenth-century polygamy (how could there be?), plural marriage in Dr. Mattie's time was more *Sister Wives* than *Sons of Perdition*, more *Three Wives* than *Leaving Bountiful*.

Victorian-era Mormon women wore the fashions of the day—not skinny jeans but not pastel prairie dresses, either. Before the railroad arrived, they made do the best they could with what could be stitched up at home. Fitz-Hugh Ludlow of the *Atlantic* described their "plebeian tweed and calico," festooned with jewelry and feathers, and "pretty girls swimming about in tasteful whip-syllabub of puffed tarlatan." (A whip-syllabub is a concoction of whipped cream, wine and sugar. There are plenty of recipes for it on the internet. It sounds delicious.) Once the railroad arrived, Utah fashionistas could buy the latest styles as soon as they could be shipped via train. As for hairdos, Dr. Mattie wore her hair short and curly, an unusual choice for her day. She would not have countenanced the long, braided, Gibson Girl up-do required in the supposedly traditional polygamous sects today.

As already discussed, polygamous wives in the 1800s not only worked in the world but were encouraged to do so. Polygamous husbands were expected to support their wives and children to the best of their ability; although, obviously, ability varied a lot. Some girls married in their teens; others, like Mattie Hughes, waited until they were finished with their education.

But really, did it work? Before Woodruff ended it, it kind of did.

12

HAPPIFY YOUR WIVES

After the Honeymoon, Before the Divorce

Polygamy is alright when properly carried out," said the daughter of polygamist Jedediah Grant, "on a shovel."

Her quip didn't speak for the Mormon majority—at the time. Most were trying mightily to figure out how to carry out polygamy—and not on a shovel. Every couple took their own approach. There were as many variations of plural marriages as there are grains of sand on the shores of the Great Salt Lake. Well, not quite, but you get the idea.

Wives close in age generally got along better. A large age gap led to resentment both ways. The older wife resented the young wife's youth and beauty; the younger wife resented the older woman's authority and experience. Age gaps also disrupted community harmony. Single men didn't begrudge their older neighbors the right to marry older women and widows, but they didn't appreciate having to compete for women their own age. Male midlife crisis being a thing back then just as it is now, older men didn't let the young men stop them. Heber C. Kimball, described by the *Atlantic* as "the jolly apostle," said, "A man who has but one wife…soon begins to wither and dry up, while a man who gives into plurality looks fresh, young, and sprightly." Angus Cannon didn't play in the kiddie pool, but he agreed with Heber on that.

First wives found it harder to adjust to polygamy, but they could flaunt their higher status. Since the vast majority of Mormons didn't engage in polygamy, it was a little naïve but not unreasonable for a first wife to expect monogamy. A second wife sometimes came as a huge blow. Second, third and fourth wives should have had no such expectations, but Mattie Hughes was certifiably miffed when Angus married his fifth wife, Maria Bennion. On the other hand, a male polygamist had higher status in Zion, and that reflected back on his wives, the first wife especially. Dr. Mattie's infatuation with Angus made her agree to be his fourth wife, but within just a few years, she'd come to realize she would have been better off as a first wife.

Marrying sister wives—as in actual sisters—was also a successful strategy. After all, sisters who had grown up together knew each other better than anyone else. Joseph Smith married Emily and Eliza Partridge in 1843. Angus Cannon's first two wives were sisters he married on the same day in 1858 (when Mattie Hughes was a babe in arms—just saying).

Angus's favorite of the two, Amanda Mousley, described their wedding day: "I was married to Mr. Cannon on July 18, 1858; was present at his marriage to my sister Sarah; the ceremony with her was completed first; we all stood up together; I think there were others present; President Young performed the ceremonies."

PEOPLING ZION WAS A principal goal for theological and practical reasons. Babies were "jewels in one's crown of glory in heaven" and were necessary to "swell the ranks of the Mormon priesthood" in the here and now. No matter his open-mindedness on women working, Brigham Young insisted a woman's primary duty was to bear children. God urged his people to "multiply and replenish," although Salt Lake City had yet to be plenished in the first place. (It had not been plenished with white Mormons, that is. The Utes were there first.)

How were the Mormons to populate Zion without wearing out the women? Even in the monogamous gentile world, women were birthing more babies than they actually wanted. The Cult of True Womanhood frowned on "lives of excessive childbearing." Nineteenth-century gentile health experts noted that continual pregnancies led to high rates of stillbirths, sickly infants and maternal malnourishment. This is not to mention that childbirth was dangerous. Puerperal fever killed. Even if a woman survived birth, long labors ended in disabling fistulas, like the one Dr. Mattie stitched up in Michigan. Because sheep gut broke and gunpowder tea almost always failed, True Women were supposed to space their babies by abstaining, but husbands didn't always take no for an answer.

In Mormondom, a polygamous husband could maximize his reproductive potential while allowing each wife to space out her pregnancies. Compared to modern women (who can choose between the pill, an implant or an IUD), polygamous wives had a lot of babies but not nearly as many as they might have in a monogamous gentile marriage. Angus Cannon's first two wives had an impressive number of children: Sarah had six, and Amanda had ten. His later wives had fewer. Clara birthed three, although only one survived. Mattie had three children. Maria had either two, three or four, depending on who's counting. The researchers at the renowned LDS Family Search say she had "at least" four, so we'll go with that. Johanna had just one, a daughter, who died in infancy.

Spacing didn't necessarily mean there were fewer babies per woman. Historical statistics suggest that the polygamists' average of 7.75 births per woman was about the same as the average of monogamists. Still, it's better to space those 7.75 babies out over twenty years rather than going hell bent for leather and dropping dead from the effort. Secondly, the more wives a husband had, the fewer births there were per wife. A second wife didn't make much difference. After three or more, it mattered.

Sometimes, theology and Zion-building ran smack-dab against the reality of money. Fed up with poverty, the sixteen-year-old daughter of polygamist Charles Johnson barred her father's entry to her mom's bedroom, saying, "You have to sleep in the barn. There are enough mouths to feed in this family."

Mattie Cannon's three children were spaced apart by five and nine years, and she had zero interest in having a gigantic family. She told Beatrice Webb of the British Fabian Society that polygamy allowed a woman to have "one or two children" with a "really good man." She scoffed at the whole "sex is only for procreation" notion. "I sometimes wonder, however, how many children would be born into the world, if the desire for offspring alone was the only incentive to the act preceding conception," she wrote to Angus. "Even our Sisters when they (many of them) find themselves 'caught,' they wish in their hearts that it had been a 'miss' instead of a 'hit.' (I speak from experience.)"

After being elected to the Utah State Senate, Mattie told the press, "Someday there will be a law compelling people to have no more than a certain amount of children and the mothers of the land can live as they ought to live."

ONE HOUSE EACH WORKED best for plural wives. Imagine getting two women to agree on the color of the curtains. It was better if the houses were close together. Angus Cannon's first two wives lived in separate houses on the same lot, which was very common. Still today, "sister wife houses" remain

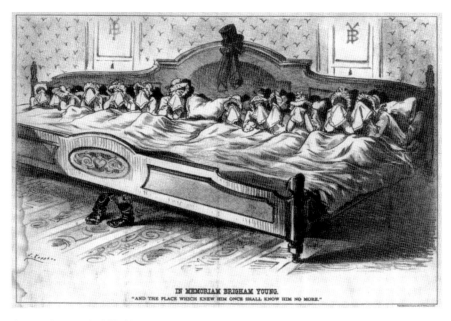

Cartoonists mocked Utah's polygamy. *Library of Congress, LC-USZ62-89570.*

slotted into backyards throughout Salt Lake City's older neighborhoods. The municipal government calls them "auxiliary dwelling units."

Sometimes, a couple wives would share a house while the other sister wives lived separately. Husbands alternated between homes for overnight visits and meals. Angus Cannon apparently preferred to eat and sleep with his favorite wife, Amanda, who shared a house with his third wife, Clara, and "visit" his other wives. Brigham Young's multi-bedroomed Lion House and its adjoining Beehive House were the exception, not the rule. (Grown women aren't keen on dorm life. And the Mormons didn't do harems, never mind what the gentile pornographers imagined. Yes, that's right. Victorian porno writers called on those exotic Mormons in far-away Utah as inspiration for their titillating tales. Why wouldn't they?)

FIRST WIVES SOMETIMES ACTUALLY sought out second and third wives for their husbands, especially if they saw the polygamy thing coming their way eventually. They might as well get it over with instead of having a "bit o' raspberry" sprung on them after being all worn out from years of doing everything all by themselves. Some single wives were lonely and wanted the company. Scandinavian emigrants sometimes asked for a Scandinavian sister wife, so they'd have somebody to talk to. First wives who failed to conceive might recruit a new wife to give her husband children, and she might even take another's child for herself in a kind of primitive, noncommercial surrogacy deal. Most ingenious of all were the wives who understood that "in union there is strength" and sought out a new wife to build an alliance against the husband or against the husband's favorite wife.

Freedom was another attraction for women. "A plural wife is not half the slave as a single wife," Senator Martha Hughes Cannon told *San Francisco Examiner* gossip columnist Annie Laurie. "If her husband has four wives, she has three weeks of freedom every single month." Echoing across the centuries, one of Enoch's wives in the BBC documentary *Three Wives* said, "If you're the fourth wife of a man, you'll still get *lots* of independence." A wife in TLC's documentary *Sister Wives* told her interviewer: "Having the lifestyle and having him only once every third night frees up a lot of time for us to do what we need to do."

"HAPPIFY" YOUR WIVES, BRIGHAM Young urged Mormon men, which may be the greatest advice ever.

As you might guess, not all polygamous wives felt all that happified. Jealousy, neglect, unromantic husbands, cruelty, financial strain, boredom and all the things that plague monogamous couples plagued polygamists, too. Some wives just fell in love with other men. Divorce, then and now, was the way out of a dissatisfying marriage. But back in the days under Joseph Smith, our friend Udney Hay Jacob, the First Prophet's misogynist spokesperson, had this to say: "When God made the woman he gave her to the man; but he never gave the man to the woman. Therefore the woman has no power to divorce the man. How can property divorce its owner?"

How, indeed? Well, Udney's logic did not survive the trek across the Great Plains. Instead of banning the practice, territorial Utah loosened it up. Mormondom offered the most permissive, female-friendly divorces in the country. Either spouse could divorce on the grounds of general unhappiness. A wife could get a divorce on the grounds that she couldn't get along with her sister wife or wives. Feminist pioneers Elizabeth Cady Stanton and Susan B. Anthony praised Mormon divorce reform.

During the nineteenth century, almost three-quarters of divorces in Utah were initiated by the wife. "For a man to seek a divorce is almost unheard of," Apostle George Q. Cannon, Angus's brother, said in 1879. "The liberty upon this point rests with the woman, and as regards a Separation, if her position should become irksome, or distasteful to her, even, and she should desire a Separation, not only is the man bound to respect the expressal of her wish to that effect, but he is bound also to give her and her offspring a proportionate share of his whole property."

Take that, Udney Hay Jacob!

Brigham Young granted 1,645 divorces. He blamed the husbands for not happifying their wives. At one point, he threatened to stop all sealings if the men didn't shape up. Unfortunately, he had some shaping up to do himself. Four of Brigham Young's wives left or divorced him.

Unlike women in the gentile world, Utah women who left their marriages weren't impoverished or ostracized. They could keep their property and their children and claim financial support from their exes. They had plenty of opportunities to remarry or be sealed anew to more righteous men. This wasn't at all like the practice of the modern fundamentalist sect of Warren Jeffs of *Keep Sweet: Pray and Obey* fame, who "reassigned" wives. In the Second Prophet's day, women could reassign themselves, and they did.

Easy divorce for women made a lot of practical sense for the Latter-day Saints of frontier days. Eternal sealings without the possibility of divorce would have had a chilling effect on marriage. It's one thing to commit "till death do us part," but who wants to be stuck with a jerk past death into "all eternity"? The deliberately under-educated women in today's creepiest fundamentalist sects, such as the one profiled in *Leaving Bountiful*, are stuck in a way their educated and economically empowered ancestral mothers never were.

Husbands rarely filed for divorce. For a man who believed his eternal exaltation depended on a multitude of wives, divorce was a religious failure. And why bother? Among the saints, a father's commitment to his children was never absolved, regardless of his relationship to their mother. If Dad didn't like Mom anymore, he could just stop "visiting." There was no need for a divorce before taking another wife or just redistributing his time.

Divorce in the gentile world remained next to impossible for women. In Utah Territory's early history, divorce was mostly a church issue. Once it was codified, Zion's easy-going statute turned the territory into a divorce mill for gentiles. (A Victorian Vegas without slot machines.)

Dr. Martha Paul Hughes Cannon never divorced Angus. They're buried together in the Salt Lake Cemetery and, if their religious beliefs prove true, will spend eternity together. On Earth, their marriage had its challenges, but Mattie was happified enough to stick with Angus Cannon for better or for worse.

The worst of it arrived just after their honeymoon.

13

POLLS, PREGNANCY AND PERSECUTION

Mattie Flees to Europe

Suffrage for women in territorial Utah was at first an example of bi-religious, nonpartisan enthusiasm. Mormons and non-Mormons agreed with equal exuberance but for different reasons. Women will vote out polygamy, gentiles fantasized. "Let the milliners and dressmakers have full sway, and they will soon make it impossible for a man to have more than one wife," is how Jennie Anderson Froiseth put it. Mormons knew better. They were relying on their milliners and dressmakers to shield the LDS's political majority against the influx of gentiles arriving on the transcontinental railroad. Losing their statewide majority was highly unlikely. (It hasn't even happened yet, and we're in another millennium.) Still, it was better to be safe than sorry. The Democratic, Republican and People's Parties all salivated over a new pool of voters to bring to their side.

Mattie Hughes had been just thirteen years old in 1870, when the Utah Territorial Legislature voted unanimously (how often does *that* happen?) to let women vote. She went through young adulthood fully expecting to cast her ballot at the polls alongside men. By the time she was of age, she had moved to Michigan, which wasn't nearly as progressive as Utah. Michigan women didn't get the right to vote until 1918. Mattie returned home to Utah in time to vote in 1884.

Congress, which oversaw the territories, saw this as an experiment in women's suffrage, which women all over the country were petitioning for, marching for and generally making themselves a nuisance for. The *Washington Chronicle* explained Congress's reasoning: "[I]f the project succeeds the right of suffrage can be extended to the sex elsewhere; but if it does not, it is only the 'Mormons' who will suffer; they will have all the trouble, and the people of the East can look calmly on until the question is settled." (Wyoming Territory actually granted women's suffrage first, but Utah made for a better experiment. Wyoming men outnumbered women six to one.) Another argument in support, one that was met with even more "decided favor" among the men in Washington, D.C., was that women voters would solve the "vexed question" of polygamy, "which all measures yet tried had failed to destroy."

It didn't work.

Women's suffrage became yet another measure that failed to destroy polygamy. Those wretched women refused to live up to expectations. They did not vote like their husbands, and they did not vote to end polygamy. Peeved at being called "degraded" by anti-Mormons, Mormon women used their enfranchisement to show the rest of the country that they were anything but. Eliza Snow told Utah women, "Your vote counts as much, weighs as heavily, as President Young's."

The 1871 *Phrenological Journal* was amazed. "Utah is the land of marvels. She gives us, first, polygamy, which seems to be an outrage against 'woman's rights,' and then offers to the nation a Female Suffrage Bill....Was there ever a greater anomaly known in the history of society?"

Good question. Was there?

DAMN UNPREDICTABLE WOMEN—NEVER TO be trusted! Their ploy having turned into a complete flop, the men in Congress got back to work. It took a while. Washington, D.C., has never been known for efficiency. In 1882, Congress passed the Edmunds Act, making polygamy and "cohabitation" a felony in the territories. Not satisfied, a follow-up, the Edmunds-Tucker Act, required voters and officeholders to swear an anti-polygamy oath.

Federal agents went window-peeping. They bribed children to tattle on their parents. Doctors like Mattie worried about being forced to turn in their patients. "Co-hab hunting" became a sport for non-Mormons. Spotters stalked people. Adult "skunks" got $20 (about $500 today) to turn in their neighbors. Plural wives hid in barns, cellars, granaries, safe houses and church steeples. Their husbands were told to run, and they did, huddling in "polygamy pits" in the Wasatch Mountains.

Mormon polygamists hid in the Wasatch Mountains above Salt Lake City. *Getty Museum.*

In 1885, Mormon women sent President Cleveland a letter objecting to the ruthlessness of federal agents (the same snarky letter that dissed "paramours," of which Cleveland himself was the most infamous) but to no avail. By way of thanks, Congress stripped them of the right to vote in 1887.

Between 1882 and 1890, 1,300 polygamists were imprisoned, including Angus. He was arrested for "lascivious co-habitation" in January 1885, three months after his wedding to Mattie. A federal deputy marshal, "armed with a pocketful of subpoenas," according to the *Deseret News,* barged into Amanda and Clara's home. Mattie wasn't there, but Amanda was ill. The deputy not only made "an abrupt and ungentlemanly entrance," but he also "rested his arm familiarly on the arm of the lady's chair." Worst of all, he leaned in so close, she could smell his "foul breath." Amanda refused to cooperate.

The marshals had better luck with Angus Jr. Amanda's twenty-three-year-old son didn't do his father any favors in court the next day, giving damning evidence right and left. By his own account, he and his father experienced "a difficulty" between each other, probably because Junior liked his liquor too much. The *Doctrine & Covenants* forbid "strong drink," but Junior admitted, "I don't know what I may have done when I was drunk." (Who does?)

The morals of the story: (1) lawbreakers, avoid pissing off your sons; (2) law enforcement, carry breath mints; (3) sons, don't get drunk.

Long story short, Angus pleaded guilty and was sent to prison with a farewell party and serenade by the Mormon Tabernacle Choir. He served six months with "vile men" (his words), murderers and forty-eight other polygamists.

Upon his release, Angus was in danger of being rearrested (and he was—more than once). Mattie had managed to avoid testifying, but she was evidence walking on two feet. She was pregnant with Angus Cannon's child. Not only that, but she could also be subpoenaed to testify against other fathers whose babies she had delivered.

"To me, it was a serious matter," she wrote, "to jail a father upon whom a lot of little children are dependent, whether those children were begotten by the same or different mothers—the fact remains they all have little mouths and must be fed."

Mattie hid out with friends until her daughter Elizabeth was born. Then she fled. She was gone for two years.

> *The gallant ship is under way*
> *To bear us off to sea.*
> *And yonder floats the streamers gay*
> *That says she waits for "we."*
> *The seamen dip the ready oar*
> *As rippling waves oft tell*
> *They bear us swiftly from the shore*
> *Our native land farewell.*

Mattie copied the words of the old Mormon hymn in her farewell letter to Angus, changing "me" to "we" and "My" to "Our" because she was taking the infant Elizabeth with her. The overland trip from Utah to New York took them less than four days on the railroad, compared to the months it had taken Mattie's family to walk (in the opposite direction) when she was a child. Now aboard ship, still fresh and naïve, they began their adventure to England.

Mattie's early letters home to her husband are admirably chirpy, all things considered. Only a few days before Mattie left Utah, Angus married Maria Bennion. Imagine, Mattie was packing to take their baby into exile, away from everyone she knew and every place familiar to her, to protect Angus from further prosecution for polygamy, and he, just months out of prison, takes wife number five! Plainly, the moral and legal cudgels the federal officials were using against polygamists were not working.

Not only that, but Maria was also the same age as Mattie. Angus's first, second and third wives were much older. Mattie, even though she was pushing thirty, apparently imagined she would have a special place as the young wife. She was no fan of Maria.

Still, Mattie enjoyed the rippling waves and the shipboard trip to England. Upon disembarking in "Merrie Olde England," Mattie reported to LDS mission headquarters in Liverpool and then headed off to live with her non-Mormon aunt and uncle in Birmingham, but she socialized with other Mormon "undergrounders"—that is, polygamists hiding out overseas—in order to get away from the cousins who terrorized baby Lizzie, not to mention her "boozer" (Mattie's word) aunt. She lied to her gentile aunt and uncle about being married. They eventually figured it out, which did not end well.

Mattie and Lizzie moved to Wolverton, where things weren't much better. "No one here eats but drink like fish," she told Angus. "You have no idea to what excess they carry it, and constantly guzzling so many malt preparations down."

Mattie didn't care for English food, either. (Who does?) "I am paying a fair price for board and lodging and am fed mainly on rusty bacon and 'bread and scrape' and not enough of that." To top it off, "there are some filthy places around here." Baby Lizzie fell ill with what Mattie called "sewer poisoning." Mattie was getting a down-and-dirty and undelicious lesson about why her family left.

If all that weren't enough to ruin a good adventure, she had to sit and listen to anti-Mormons dis her own husband! Somehow, these Englanders had heard about Angus's arrest. (News travels, especially news of polygamy.) Anxious not to blow her cover, "Maria Munn," as Mattie called herself (Munn was Angus's middle name), chimed in that she was "not much acquainted with him, but guessed he was sort of a doughhead as they selected that sort to make president of stakes." At least, that's how she reported this remarkable conversation back to the doughhead himself.

When she got tired of the name Maria Munn, Mattie signed her letters "Emma Quirk," "Maria Quirk" and even "Ezekial Brown." She addressed Angus as "James," "Dearest" and "Old Duck."

Old Duck wasn't as cagey at obscuring his identity. Mattie scolded him for using the word *wife* in his letters. What's the point of hiding out across the ocean when your husband sends incriminating evidence through the mail? "Dearest, please refrain, until we meet, then whisper in my ear, and read in my eyes how I love to hear it," she wrote, so sweetly.

MONEY WAS TIGHT. DR. Cannon figured out right away that the English were too poor to pay for her medical skills. Unable to work for money, Mattie visited hospitals to observe. She was not impressed. (This was decades before Britain's National Health Service.) Angus had to send her funds. She was vexed at having to write home for permission to take trips to Paris and London. "I'll pay you back every cent," she begged (the underlining is hers). She waffled between expecting his financial support (being his wife who was exiled on his behalf) and offering to reimburse him (being a woman with the means to support herself).

"I have become an expensive addition to your charges," she wrote, perhaps disingenuously. "But when I get back to work I will return every cent I have had from you. Does that make you mad? I remember you telling me once that a woman loved a man more when he supported her."

On second thought, not perhaps, she was definitely being disingenuous.

BAD HEALTH ANNOYED MATTIE throughout her exile in Europe. At first, she thought she was pregnant again.

"If I am 'on the road to glory' again, the thing occurred between two and three months ago," she wrote to Angus in June 1886. "If other things have not pressed too heavily on your memory, you probably recollect."

She planned to return to the United States to give birth, so if it was a boy, he could become president. She extended to Angus a "cordial invitation to be present on the occasion." Alas, there was no reason to return home. She was not pregnant.

Instead, she suffered from vaginal prolapse and what appears to have been a chronic urinary tract infection. Vaginal prolapse can be a side effect of childbirth, and it feels like one is sitting on a ball. In October, she took to wearing a pessary, a device to support her "dilapidated womb." (Her words again.) Even though she didn't like to be seen as a "chronic grunter," she also complained to Angus about her headaches, probably migraines.

Mattie's English doctor advised that she should "on no account" become pregnant again, which would have been a particular blow to a Mormon wife—or maybe not. For all the cute names Mattie gave her baby (Cherub, Our Little Peach Blossom, Little Traveler and Our Treasure), Lizzie was no fun and games companion. She cried from teething, weaning, measles, a cough. At one point, she drank a vial of ammonia Mattie kept for cleaning clothing. Thankfully, Mormon "consecrated oil" (olive oil that had been blessed) worked as an emetic, and she survived. Lizzie was also clingy, which was understandable, all things considered, but this made for an added burden on a mother with a prolapsed uterus. Mattie also worried that Lizzie wasn't bonding with Angus. She showed the baby a photograph of "her pa." Lizzie licked it.

Mattie reported this all home with her characteristic snark, what the Victorians would have called "eating vinegar with a fork." She wrote to Angus: "I don't think you'll find me lashing myself into jealous rages if you see fit to take additional young wives for eternity and to propagate the species, as I have come to the conclusion that I am totally unfit for the work, & must be content to see others do it."

ANGUS HAD TROUBLES OF his own back home in Utah. After getting out of prison in December 1885, he lay low (not counting marrying a fifth wife), what the *Salt Lake Democrat* called "skulking" and the LDS's *Deseret News* described as appearing in public "only when his duty positively required it."

By November 1886, he'd gotten word that federal officials weren't after him anymore, so he decided to take his son John deer hunting. This was a bad idea. Law enforcement spotted his buggy and rearrested him. Bond was set at the extraordinarily high $10,000. He quipped, "I seem to be increasing in value; I was only worth $1,500 a year ago."

There would be no guilty plea this time. This time, he'd stick it in their eye. As soon as he was bonded out, Angus preached a rabble-rousing sermon before a packed crowd in the tabernacle: "I look forward…to the time when I can embrace the mothers of my children, and when I can associate with the children whose pale faces I now see watching on the streets for their father," he proclaimed.

The crowd included gentile reporters. The *Salt Lake Democrat* was not moved: "His sermon was one of those rambles in which he takes such delight.…True to his nature, Angus repeated the assertion that he gloried in having been caught.…Taking all he has said it would be hard to tell what Angus does glory in; but there's no denying it, he is glad about something and he wants it distinctly understood." The review in the *Deseret News* was less snarky and even less comprehensible.

In December 1886, his case went to preliminary hearing. It was the show of shows. A crowd of the curious jammed in, expecting to hear salacious testimony from over thirty witnesses. The main charge was "co-habitation" with both Sarah Cannon (his first wife) and Mattie Hughes (who was nowhere to be found), with additional charges of co-habiting with Amanda Mousley, Clara Moses, Maria Bennion and Hattie Harker.

Prosecutor Dickson "came in with the bustling air of the last party at a duel," according to the *Salt Lake Herald*. He put Mattie's mother on the stand. She testified that Mattie had been "called away professionally" and said she didn't know where Mattie had gone or how long she'd be gone, which may or may not have been perjury. Mattie's half-sister Barbara Paul testified that she hadn't known Mattie was going to leave the country but that "she can take care of herself." Also testifying were Mattie's half-brother, Joshua Paul; her sister wife Amanda; Kate Cannon, a daughter-in-law of a sister wife who gave some damning testimony she retracted the next day; Angus Jr., the drunken son who'd botched his testimony so badly the year before (he did better this second time around); a Dr. Belle Anderson, who swore Mattie had not been pregnant; Elizabeth Owen (the lady whose morphine Mattie spotted and whose lounge she slept on); plus a slew of others.

The most damning and sensational testimony was supposed to come from a young Englishman named Robert Parsons, who was purported to have told his drinking buddy Mr. Pratt and federal marshal F.H. Dyer that he'd peeped into a window at the hospital "out of curiosity" and seen Mattie and Angus in bed together. At the hearing, he denied it. "I do not remember the conversation with Mr. Dyer," he testified, "though being hurt several times I am affected in the head, and when I drink whisky I am not responsible for what I say." He did recall having "two or three doses of whisky" the night he was drinking and yakking with Dyer. The gallery was amused and the prosecutor disgusted. Mr. Parsons was excused.

The last straw was the testimony of Angus Cannon's alleged wife and university teacher Hattie Harker. She denied being married to Angus and then "sailed out of the room, leaving Mr. Dickson's underpinnings knocked in confusion about the floor," in the words of the *Salt Lake Herald*.

It's possible that was the only true testimony of the day. Hattie Harker was not one of Angus's wives.

All charges against Angus were dropped, or, as the *Deseret News* put it with delightful Victorian swagger, "[T]he whole expensive, vexatious, and bombatious business is a complete fizzle."

EXILED IN EUROPE, MATTIE made the best of it—for a while. "I have ascended some of the highest towers and descended into some of the darkest dungeons of England with the little bunch of living, breathing humanity in my arms, and found it genuine hard work, at least it made my back ache fearfully." But she was determined to "lose no opportunity to learn, see and enjoy."

It was not all hard work. She tried to gin up some jealousy in Angus, writing home about one particular dungeon-descending tour guide who was "handsome and gallant," a "young" and "fine fellow." She also decided to dye her hair and was quite proud of the result. She wrote to Angus that

Mattie fled to England for two years. *Library of Congress, LC-DIG-stereo-1s22881.*

he should do "like I have done which has...presented the opportunity for several flirtations, did I desire to take advantage of them. I guess it was the hair dye, as I don't think engaging fellows would smile on an old gray-headed woman." She was thirty when she wrote that; Angus was fifty-three.

In 1887, Angus and Amanda's son Lewis sailed over on a mission trip to Switzerland. He, Mattie and Lizzie played tourist together. Mattie joked that she did not know which wife was Lewis's mother (or maybe she was serious), but it hardly mattered. They were relatively close in age and enjoyed a "period of enchantment," touring the art galleries, palaces, gardens and boulevards of Paris. Switzerland, on the other hand, was "rediculous [*sic*]." She didn't specify exactly what she found so ridiculous. The lederhosen? Yodeling? Those twelve-foot-long Alpine horns?

She marveled at how much coffee the Swiss drank and wondered "how it is that we discard that staple of diet." (Poor Lewis was trying to convince the Swiss to take up polygamy *and* give up coffee.)

Swiss snoopiness was another irritation. They kept asking why so many Mormon wives were hanging out in Switzerland and why they were there for so long. When it got to be too much, Mattie's Mormon friend "Anna" made up a story that there was a U.S. law that forbade women from having babies less than three years apart. (There was no such law, but Mattie didn't necessarily disagree with the concept.)

When Lewis eventually set to his mission work, Mattie and Lizzie returned to England.

As HER EXILE DRAGGED on, Mattie ate her vinegar with a fork more often. Salutations like "My Own Loved One" turned into "Dear Munn." She "grunted" that exile was a "dreary desert" and lamented that she was "wedded, yet experiencing none of the elements of <u>true</u> wedded life." It couldn't have helped that Angus married wife number six, Johanna Danielson, while Mattie was overseas.

Where Mattie had once urged Angus to "imagine yourself kissed, hugged, and a piece taken out of your ear," a year later, she lectured, "Don't you think it a pity you took time to marry the woman who now expects you to spend one out of one hundred and sixty-eight hours of the week in writing to her?"

It's true Angus didn't write often, and when he did, he was not nearly so bombastic as when he preached to the Latter-day Saints in the tabernacle. The guy was wracked with guilt—and not without good reason. "I am in a poor position to judge of your circumstances and what you need," he wrote in July 1887. "It is, as you have said, hard for me to put myself in the place of one banished, amongst strangers, unto a strange land, for the good of another, and I that other, surrounded by a large family and many in whom I have an interest."

He rued his parsimony, too. "I thought you could go anywhere and do anything with very little money, which is another evidence of my unreasonableness and simplicity."

"I SHOULD GO MAD if I continued this life much longer," Mattie wrote to Angus, depressed and despairing near the end of 1887, "cooped in doors with a fretful baby.…[Male acquaintances] are here in London and are going everywhere—theatres, museums, art galleries and everywhere—While I can't take babe out on account of fog nor can I leave her." (She was referring to the yellow fog, London's poisonous sulphur dioxide.)

"While I have been writing this she has had my button box, spilt its contents all over the floor, pulled the thread all off its spool, pulled my writing material all over, and spilt the ink and is now fairly raving for more entertainment—the most nervous fractious child you ever saw in your life." If you've ever dealt with a toddler, you get it. The terrible twos are fractious on foot. Mattie was dealing with it all on her own and had come to believe that Angus didn't love her and maybe never had.

Deep "in the morbs," as Victorians called depression, Mattie dined one night with some Mormon brethren. Out of the blue, she "burst out into a violent paroxysm of crying," which "rather astonished them." Fortunately, things had settled down in Utah, and she was preparing to go home.

In December, Mattie and Lizzie boarded ship. Angus met them at the pier in New York City. They spent several days together but had to split up again. After two years of suffering vaginal prolapse while dragging about a fractious child, Mattie wanted the best medical treatment she could find. That meant going back to Michigan. Angus returned to his other five wives and their children.

For Mattie, it turned out to be a wise move. Whatever the Michigan doctors did, it worked. Never mind the English doctor's advice, when she finally returned to Utah, she became pregnant again and gave birth to her son James in 1890.

That was the manifesto year, the year everything changed for polygamous Mormons.

14

MARRIAGE? BAH HUMBUG!

The Victorian Free Lovers and Non-Lovers

Open your silverware drawer, turn over a fork or a spoon and read the inscription. It's a safe bet it says "Oneida" or "Oneida Community." No? Double or nothing. Ask your mom what's on the back of hers.

What we know today as a stainless-steel flatware manufacturing company—a super successful one at that—started out as a Victorian free love commune. If you think Mormon polygamists were eccentric, you're going to love the Oneidans.

SELFISHNESS AND INEQUALITY ARE the roots of human misery, the Oneidans believed, along with unwanted pregnancy and too much laundry. (Methinks they weren't wrong.) Led by the befreckled, ginger-headed and super-religious John Humphrey Noyes, a small group of exceptionally open-minded Victorians designed a community to fix all that.

One man/one woman marriage was selfish, so out the door it went! In its place, the Oneidans put "complex marriage," in which all the women in the community were married to all the men in the community. Biblical communism, sharing room, board and labor, equalized everybody's economic status and elevated their standard of living. Men practiced "coitus reservatus" to prevent unwanted pregnancies. The women shucked off their thirty-seven-pound fashion ensemble and put in its place a long blouse and comfy pantaloons. On laundry day, both men and women pitched in to help.

Men and women worked laundry day at Oneida. *iStock.*

And there you have it—heaven on Earth!

Unless you include the Mormons of Utah, the Oneida Community in Upstate New York was the most notorious, successful and longest-lived commune of the Victorian utopia craze. A lot of folks were unhappy with the way the world was turning out and tried all sorts of new ways of living and new ways of having and not having sex. The century birthed the celibate Shakers and Rappites, free love Fouriers and the communalists in Amana, Iowa (of eventual microwave fame)—and many others.

Most nineteenth-century utopias lasted just a few years. Three hundred or so Oneidans lived their communal, free love lifestyle for over three decades before they turned their community into a flatware factory. Their ninety-three-thousand-square-foot Community Mansion House, a red-brick mega-dorm in the Italianate style, stands today as a National Historic Landmark.

CASANOVA OR A SAINT? Like Joseph Smith, John Humphrey Noyes was a mixed bag. Inspired by Jesus's admonition recorded in Matthew 5:48 ("Be ye perfect, even as your Father in heaven is perfect."), John Humphrey preached perfectionism, a belief that Christians can be freed from sin in this life on

Earth. His brand of perfectionism identified "making twain of one flesh" as a spiritually enlightening act, provided it was done *outside* of traditional marriage.

Before his enlightenment, Noyes had traditionally married Harriet Holton in 1838. Their first foray into what would become complex marriage came in Putney, Vermont, in 1846. They were basically wife-swapping with their friends George and Mary Cragin. (Just try to imagine how that initial conversation got going.) Within a few months, they'd expanded what they called "four square marriage" to include Noyes's sisters and their husbands. Like Joseph Smith's secret polygamy (which was going on at the same time), "complex marriage" was kept under the covers and in the dark.

Still, secrets get out. Rumors (true as they were) ping-ponged around Putney. Arrest warrants were issued. Just as the Mormons got driven from New York to the Midwest and then on to Utah, Noyes and his little band of lovers decided it was a good idea to hightail it out of Vermont. In 1848, they moved to the heretic's paradise of Upstate New York, the home of the Shakers and the birthplace of Mormonism. Persecution didn't dampen their enthusiasm or deprive them of converts. By the end of the year, 84 people had signed away all their belongings to join the Oneida Community. At its height, Oneida housed 230 to 300 believers. There were branch communities in Brooklyn, New York, and Walling, Connecticut.

"Sticky love" was forbidden. Exclusive pairings led to jealousy and quarreling, "impediments to harmony." Traditional marriage "provokes adultery, actual or of the heart." Noyes would roll over in his grave to find out his Oneida campus is today a wedding venue.

COMPARISONS TO MORMONISM WERE inevitable. Presbyterian minister and morality crusader John W. Mears had this to say: "The people of Illinois could not endure the immorality of the Mormons, but drove them from Nauvoo in 1846 and compelled them to take refuge in the Great Basin, a thousand miles from the outskirts of civilization. Thus polygamy was treated; while the far more corrupt concubinage of the Oneida community luxuriates at ease in the heart of New York State." John Humphrey Noyes was compared to Brigham Young. The *New York Observer* denounced the Oneida Community as "united adulterers," adding a backhanded compliment to the Mormons, who at least held to "the distinction of husband and wife."

The comparisons were not totally off the mark. Both Mormons and Oneidans considered their sexual systems ordained by God. Both embraced selflessness as a sacred goal. A Mormon polygamist explained, "There is nothing in the world so good as polygamy to make people unselfish." Mormon Relief Society president Zina Jacobs Smith Young called exclusive, romantic love "a false sentiment."

Where the two communities differed—utterly—was their attitude toward procreation. Mormon polygamy conceived many babies, while Oneidan complex marriage produced very few.

How to enjoy "amative sex" while avoiding "propagative sex" was a challenge John Humphrey Noyes took seriously. He and Harriet had one living son, Theodore, but had also endured the grief of four stillbirths. They would do anything to avoid a fifth. His many hours of Bible reading convinced him that withdrawal (the so-called "sin of Onan") was "sowing seed by the wayside," which he believed God condemned. Catching seed in a condom seemed like a tidier way to commit the same sin. What were they to do?

Problem-solver extraordinaire John Humphrey came up with an innovative and, as it turned out, highly effective trick called coitus reservatus. In the words of Noyes's critic John B. Ellis, coitus reservatus was a practice "so curious and monstrous that I almost shrink from explaining it." (Almost!) *Curious* is a good word. *Monstrous* seems kind of harsh.

In short, men were not to climax at all, but they were supposed to make women climax as often as possible. (OK, ladies, let's hear it for John Humphrey!)

Sex was, when done correctly, like a boat ride. Here's how John Humphrey Noyes explained coitus reservatus in his euphemistically Victorian manner:

> *The skillful boatman may choose whether he will remain in the still water, or venture more or less down the rapids, or run his boat over the fall. But there is no point on the verge of the fall where he has no control over his course; and just above that there is a point where he will have to struggle with the current in a way which will give his nerves a severe trial, even though he may escape the fall. If he is willing to learn, experience will teach him the wisdom of confining his excursions to the region of easy rowing, unless he has an object in view that is worth the cost of going over the falls.*

Got that?

Turns out Oneida men were remarkably successful at struggling with the current. Among the 250-plus free-loving adults, there was only one or maybe two accidental pregnancies per year, even though, as Noyes noted, "the natural instinct of our nature demands frequent congress of the sexes." Men were not going over the falls on a regular basis. On the other hand, Oneida women were totally enjoying their partners' excursions into the region of easy rowing. If you catch the drift.

Obviously, this kind of boating took practice. Postmenopausal women trained the young guys. Once they had mastered the technique, young men could request partners their own age. Those who never mastered it, the delightfully designated "leakers," had to stick with the old broads unless a woman actually wanted a child, in which case, the object in view made it worth the cost of going over the falls.

In spite of the "free love" label, Oneida's system was not without rules. A woman could not initiate sex, although she could refuse. A third party was supposed to arrange every "congress," "experience," "connection" and "interview" (for all their free loving, the Oneidans had a typical Victorian devotion to sexual euphemisms). Records were kept. Liaisons were dutifully recorded.

And sex was always between one male and one female—no orgies! Homosexuality was also forbidden but not pedophilia. Older men, very often Noyes himself, "initiated" girls as young as thirteen (some claim even younger). Eventually, this would contribute to the sect's undoing. The other men got jealous, and the young girls were disgusted.

MEANWHILE, ONEIDA THRIVED FOR other reasons. It wasn't just about free love. They made their living manufacturing the country's best animal traps and highest-quality silk thread. All of the work, both manufacturing and domestic, including the dreaded laundry, was done by teams of mixed genders. There was neither "women's work" nor "men's work." Men ironed, and women hammered iron in the metal shop. Just like the Mormons, Oneidans described their system as a "beehive."

Intellectual development was encouraged for everyone. Noyes insisted that women were intellectual equals to men and encouraged women to "criticize men and express their own tastes and feelings." Nevertheless, for all their progressive egalitarianism, Oneidans, like Mormons, considered men *spiritually* superior.

IS SPIRITUALITY GENETIC? CAN it be bred? After two decades of coitus reservatus, this question vexed John Humphrey Noyes to the point that he decided the object in view made it worth the cost of going over the falls. He wanted the Oneidans to start making babies—and not just any babies but *spiritually superior* babies. In a quirky twist on the then-popular eugenics movement, Noyes decided the most spiritual Oneida men should impregnate the most spiritual Oneida women. Community members applied for his "stirpiculture" experiment. A committee chaired by Noyes chose fifty-three spiritually superior women and thirty-eight spiritually superior men. Foremost among them, naturally, was the most spiritually superior of all: Noyes himself.

The experiment lasted from 1869 to 1879 and produced either forty-five or fifty-eight—maybe sixty-nine—stirpicult children, depending on which historian is counting. (It's understandably difficult to separate the stirpies from the oopsies.) About a dozen were fathered by Noyes. Stirpies were raised in the Children's House, not by their parents but communally by male and female child tenders. They grew up to be quite intellectual and unusually tall (according to an 1891 study) but not particularly spiritual.

Not only did the stirpiculture experiment fail, but it backfired. Women and men didn't really like a committee deciding who was spiritual enough to conceive a child. (Go figure.) The selection of the stirpiculture parents also created an elite class, demolishing the whole concept of Oneidan equality. Plus, weird old John Humphrey was just creeping out those "jammiest bits of jam," the young women he chose as his spiritual breeders.

Adding to that was all the news about the campaign against Mormons. John Humphrey Noyes saw the persecution of Mormon polygamy as writing on the wall for the Oneidans. Getting old and in failing health, Noyes fled the community but remained adamantly opposed to traditional marriage. He suggested Oneidans become celibate. His community of rowers, both the ones who stuck to easy rowing and those who went over the falls, set a different course.

On August 28, 1879, the Oneidans voted to end complex marriage. They started getting married immediately. A year later, they transformed their commune into a company, incorporating as Oneida Community Ltd. Seeing that animal traps and silk thread were not the waves of the future, they cast about for a trendier moneymaking venture. Ironically, John Humphrey's own child Pierrepont Noyes came up with the idea of making high-quality but affordable flatware and marketing it as wedding gifts for brides.

Irony notwithstanding, the business was a huge success. Ninety years after the Oneidans abandoned free love for the free market, their stainless-steel spoons, engraved with the NASA seal, went to the moon on *Apollo 12* in 1969. Today, in the twenty-first century, online bridal registration websites still suggest Oneida flatware as a thoughtful wedding present.

John Humphrey Noyes would turn over in his grave if he saw this. *By Jon Whitcomb, 1948; public domain, via Internet Archive.*

DOZENS OF COMMUNES LITTERED the American landscape in the nineteenth century, all experimenting with different ways of living and having and not having sex: Icarians ended up planting vineyards in California; Fouriers predicted a future Age of Harmony, when the oceans would turn into lemonade and people would ride lions for high-speed transportation (apparently, jets were too hard to imagine); Shakers; Owenites; Amana colonists; Janssonites; Rappites; Harmonists; and God only knows how many others during the utopia craze. You could go crazy trying to inventory them all.

The point is that it wasn't just the Mormons who sought to build a sexually untraditional heaven on Earth. It was going on all over, and for the most part, these communes were nicer places for women than the broader American culture.

15

MATTIE MULTITASKS, FREAK STATE FEMINISTS FIGHT FOR THE VOTE

Career, motherhood, politics—Mattie hit the ground running when she finally returned to Salt Lake City in 1888. Within six months, she had opened Utah's first training school for nurses. Mattie also reestablished her medical practice. And apparently, the doctors in Michigan had successfully repaired what she had described as her "dilapidated womb," because she shunted aside her English doctor's advice and got pregnant again.

Then a runaway horse tipped her carriage, and she miscarried.

On top of all this, Angus was not behaving in an especially gallant manner. It's certainly understandable that after exiling herself for two years on his behalf, Mattie expected an extra-special spot in his little pantheon of wives. But it was not to be. "How do you think I feel when I meet you driving around another plural wife about in a glittering carriage in broad daylight. I am entirely out of money…after all my sacrifice and loss you treat me like a dog—and parade others before my eyes. I will not stand it," she wrote to him.

Nevertheless, she was soon pregnant for a third time. Ignoring the era's custom of "confinement," which sentenced pregnant women to bed for the last trimester, Mattie did as she pleased. One evening, probably bored out of her mind and jealous of those other wives gadding about in that glittering carriage, Mattie disguised herself as an old (and very fat) woman and went to see the play *Josephine* at the Salt Lake Theater. Two days later, her son James was born.

It was 1890, the year of the manifesto, the year LDS president Wilford Woodruff ended polygamy—kind of. It was the year he made

Utah statehood a possibility, the year that invigorated Utah feminists to fight for the vote. They wanted to get the vote for all women—and get it back for themselves.

THE "FREAK STATES," AS Wyoming, Colorado and Idaho were called, allowed women to vote. Women in Utah Territory had voted until Congress stripped them of the right (to punish polygamists). And now, Mormon women were clamoring to get the vote back. Gentile women were more sanguine, viewing their disenfranchisement as a politically acceptable sacrifice, seeing as how it reduced Mormon political influence.

At the forefront of this suffrage movement was Emmeline Wells and the LDS newspaper she edited, the *Woman's Exponent*, whose nameplate proclaimed: "The Rights of Women of Zion, and the Rights of Women of All Nations." She didn't want Utah to just restore the vote for its own women. Her mission was to fight for "posterity [and] all women throughout the land."

Who better to enlist in this campaign than her former typesetter? The fine-looking Dr. Mattie Hughes, a Michigan-educated and beloved physician, graduate of the National School of Elocution and Oratory, mother of two and fourth wife of the president of the Salt Lake Stake?

Who better, indeed?

Times being what they were, the fourth wife thing was a problem. The *Woman's Exponent* did not refer to Mattie using the last name Cannon, even though she'd been married to Angus for years. Polygamists were still being prosecuted. In spite of that, Utahns wanted nothing more than a seat at the cool kids' table. They wanted to be a state, and it was clear as the air over the Wasatch Mountains that would never happen as long as their men were marrying multiple wives.

A new president of the Church of Jesus Christ of Latter-day Saints, Wilford Woodruff, took office in 1889. Twenty years prior, as a mere Apostle, he had warned that plucking "one feather of the bird" (ending plural marriage) would destroy the Mormon religion. Times had changed. Immediately, but quietly, the fourth president began refusing requests to conduct plural marriages in the Endowment House. (The temple was still under construction.) Then he had the Endowment House torn down.

Finally, in October 1890, he plucked the feather, announcing:

> *Inasmuch as laws have been enacted by Congress forbidding plural marriages, which laws have been pronounced constitutional by the court*

of last resort, I hereby declare my intention to submit to those laws, to use my influence with the members of the Church over which I preside to have them do likewise….I now publicly declare that my advice to the Latter-day Saints is to refrain from contracting any marriage forbidden by the law of the land.

The Woodruff Manifesto was a cataclysm. Never mind that only a small percentage of Mormondom practiced polygamy, but the revelation given to their First Prophet, Joseph Smith, was now just a feather floating away, soon to disappear over the horizon. Still, Woodruff did not kill the bird. As we know today, Woodruff definitely did not kill the bird.

No one was being asked to get a divorce or abandon their families. Angus and his fellow polygamists tried to be discreet—no more parading his plural wives in a glittering carriage. "[The manifesto] has made me more modest and I have only been as attentive as I felt common humanity required me to be," Angus explained years later. "I…have not paraded my families but in honest pride I have nourished them." For all his post-manifesto modesty, Angus was not celibate, nor did he limit himself to one wife.

Why did Woodruff do it? Was the manifesto a divine revelation or a capitulation to temporal authorities? Brigham Young's grandson Kimball nailed it in 1954, writing that polygamy had once been useful, but by 1890, it was simply not that useful anymore. The LDS Church had proved it could grow well enough without it. Zion was populated.

The manifesto didn't dissolve plural marriages and didn't even stop all the marrying. But as wishy-washy as it was, it worked the way Woodruff hoped. The bounty hunting and window peeping stopped. In 1894, President Grover Cleveland (of "Ma, Ma, Where's My Pa?" infamy) issued amnesty to polygamous husbands.

Most importantly, the manifesto made Utah statehood a possibility. Emmeline Wells, Dr. Mattie Hughes Cannon and other Mormon women bolted into action. A new state would need a constitution, and by hook or crook, the women were determined to regain the right to vote. They would lead the way for all women in the United States.

It was time for Dr. Mattie to dust off her degree in oration.

BEDAZZLING AND BODACIOUS BEST describe the 1893 Chicago's World Fair, also known as the Columbian Exposition, where Dr. Martha Hughes Cannon of Salt Lake City, Utah, was a featured speaker at the World's Congress

The first Ferris wheel carried more than two thousand people at once. *Library of Congress, LC-DIG-ds-14185.*

of Women. More than twenty-seven million people visited the 690-acre White City during its six-month run (the entire U.S. population at the time was sixty-three million), including seven thousand who came all the way from Utah.

The world's first Ferris wheel twirled there. Each of the thirty-six enclosed cars measured twenty-four feet long, thirteen feet wide and ten feet tall and contained fancy swivel chairs for the comfort of thirty-eight passengers, plus standing room for twenty-two more in each car. Do the math. The first Ferris wheel carried 2,160 people at a time. More than 34,000 people a day paid fifty cents admission to board the marvel and go twice around in twenty minutes.

At night, across the fairgrounds, ninety thousand electric bulbs sparkled inside and outside the two hundred pure white buildings. (The fairgrounds inspired Katherine Lee Bates to write "thine alabaster cities gleam" in her song "America the Beautiful." The White City was also the inspiration for the Emerald City of *Wizard of Oz* fame—not to mention Disneyland. Walt's father worked as a plasterer on the fair buildings.) Inside were exhibitions of and lectures on culture, art, anthropology, agriculture, manufacturing and science from forty-six different countries. It was nerd heaven!

Most relevant to Dr. Mattie were the Woman's Building and Utah Building. The colonnaded Woman's Building was spectacular. Designed by a woman architect, Sophia Hayden, its library showcased seven thousand books, all written by women, plus art and handicraft. There were murals by Mary Fairchild MacMonnies Low and Mary Cassatt. Cassatt's mural measured fifty-eight by twelve feet, showcasing the advancement of women through history. She painted women picking fruit, dancing and playing music. After the exhibition closed, the mural disappeared and has never been found. Fortunately, though, photographers took pictures, which you can find online.

Two pictures of Native Americans by Utah's own Kate Wells greeted visitors in the foyer of the Woman's Building. Inside was an exhibit of Mormon-made silk, including curtains and a piano scarf. Remember, it was Brigham Young who encouraged Mormon women to take up sericulture in the 1850s. The silk for these items was woven from threads spun by Utah's own silkworms, which were fed on Zion's own mulberry trees. Emma Bull created a silk and velvet crazy quilt, onto which she stitched images of the Salt Lake Temple, a log cabin, an American flag, a Union Jack, a sego lily and a beehive.

The Utah Building got ten thousand visitors a day for five months, the vast majority being non-Mormons. Notwithstanding the monumentally scaled Brigham Young statute standing guard outside, territory leaders were keen to distract folks from thinking too much about polygamy. Exhibiting a flair for public relations, the Utahns hung a ginormous American flag, sixteen feet long and four feet wide, made from the wool of Zion's own sheep. Better yet, the building's central feature was a massive, plush circular divan where

Left: Mary Cassatt's mural at the Columbian Exposition was lost. *Public Domain, via Wikimedia.*

Below: The Utah Building at the Columbian Exposition. *By permission, Utah State Historical Society.*

tired fairgoers were invited to rest their feet. Anyone who has traipsed about a large fair recognizes the genius in this. It was a thoughtful attraction, plus a subtle reminder that Mormon pioneer history made them particularly well-acquainted with the agony of sore feet.

"THE MOST WONDERFUL GATHERING of women the world has ever seen," is how the *Exponent* described the World's Congress of Women, where Mattie was a featured speaker in May 1893. Emmeline Wells extolled the congress for its "spirit of love and abundant charity and peace," uniting "women of all lands" and "women of all religions" in "great sisterhood." Wowee! Who'd want to miss *that?*

Dr. Mattie Hughes Cannon awoke the morning of May 19, 1893, in a comfortable bed at Chicago's sumptuous Palmer House Hotel. If Angus was with her or not, we don't know. Built in 1875, the seven-story Palmer House was known for its oversized rooms, luxurious décor and famous guests. The champion libertine President Grover Cleveland had slept there, as did the gay author Oscar Wilde, Mormon satirizer Mark Twain and our Civil War victor Union General Ulysses S. Grant. (The current "historic" Palmer House Hilton was built in 1923 on the same site.)

The hotel also proved its chops in the kitchen. We are all ever grateful for the special confection Palmer House bakers invented for the 1893 Columbian Exposition: the chocolate brownie. It would be sad to find out Dr. Mattie Hughes Cannon never tried one, but she certainly must have. Imagine the ravings in the lobby. "Have you tried the chocolate brownie? You must! It's bang up to the elephant!" (That's Victorian for perfect and wonderful.)

Dr. Mattie was not usually one to fuss about fashion, but on that spring morning, she got all dolled up in a green dress with a matching hat and gloves. No one in Chicago was going to accuse her of being a dowdy polygamous drudge! After breakfast, at ten o'clock or so, Mattie and the other Mormon women staying at the Palmer gathered to start their day in song. The selected hymn, written by Eliza R. Snow, "O My Father," was, despite its title, a radically feminist hymn, proclaiming God to be both male and female. The hymn ends this way:

> *Father, Mother, may I meet you*
> *In your royal courts on high?*
> *Then, at length, when I've completed*
> *All you sent me forth to do,*
> *With your mutual approbation*
> *Let me come and dwell with you.*

Mattie's swank digs at the Columbian Exposition. *Library of Congress, LC-DIG-stereo-1s43712.*

Eliza instructed the hymn to be sung "fervently." Have no doubt Mattie and the other Mormon women did just that. Another hymn they probably sang, rewritten by Lula Richards just for this event, ended thus:

Woman, rise! Thy penance o'er,
Sit thou in the dust no more;
Seize the scepter, hold the van,
Equal with thy brother, man.

Then, out to the fair!

Lectures at the World's Congress of Women were held at the magnificent Palace of Fine Arts, an architectural spectacle if there ever was one. None of the buildings at the 1893 World's Fair were built to last. They were just shells coated with a mix of plaster of paris, jute and hemp. The plan was to tear them down after the fair and recycle the iron, wood and bricks. As it was simply too magnificent to demolish as planned, the Arts Palace was left to deteriorate until it was rebuilt using more durable limestone in 1927. Today, it houses Chicago's Museum of Science and Industry.

Mattie and her women friends climbed the steps of the building and walked through the palace portico, among the Ionic columns, into this enormous and splendid building, which was nevertheless not as splendid and only half as big as the temple in Salt Lake City. When it was her turn to talk, Dr. Mattie spoke about the "types of women who live in Zion," focusing on women's strength, religious freedom and Mormon patriotism: "In following out the migrating instinct of their fore-fathers those early-day women of Utah did not forget the principles for which so much had been sacrificed to establish religious toleration on the free soil of America, for when they had reached the end of their journey they proved their patriotism and loyalty by rallying around their husbands and sons while they raised the Stars and Stripes."

MORMON MEN, SHUT OUT of this shindig, celebrated their women's success, while, at the same time, they lobbied to be included in September's Parliament of World's Religions, touted as an exhibition of "all faiths." Well, all faiths except Mormonism, Native religions and Sikhism but including Spiritualism (think Ouija boards).

Male LDS leaders were no dummies. They recognized a snub of biblical proportions, but as a matter of strategic courtesy, they pretended it was a mere clerical oversight. It's so easily corrected! No offense taken!

But no dice. The Latter-day Saints would be "a disturbing element," the organizers sniffed. While Mormon women got two full sessions in the World's Congress of Women, LDS men were shunned entirely.

Music was another matter. On September 8, 1893, the Mormon Tabernacle Choir took the stage at the Welsh Eisteddfed Festival Hall at the Columbian Exposition, winning the silver medal and a prize of $1,000 (about $30,000 today). From the audience was heard the shout, "Three cheers for the Mormons!" So, they got their day in the September sun after all.

THE GARGANTUAN WOOLEN FLAG in the Utah Building was taken down at the end of October, and the silks were packaged up. Back home in Utah, statehood was winking on the horizon, and women were anxious to get their rights back. In 1895, Mattie was on the constitutional convention's Committee of the Territorial Association of Woman Suffragists, representing "the great majority of the women of Utah."

The Territorial Association of Woman Suffragists laid out its demands, which were neither demure nor dainty and definitely not within the True Woman's "separate sphere" of home and hearth: "[W]omen should be accorded equal rights and privileges of citizenship, that sex distinction shall no longer be a ban and a bar to equal opportunity with men to exercise the God-given powers and capabilities with which women are endowed." The committee pointed out that the customary constitutional preamble "we, the people," should logically encompass women, because "[w]hatever the status of women may be, they are at least part of the people." They noted that women in Utah paid taxes as owners of properties and businesses. "Hence, the disfranchisement of half the people and a large proportion of taxpayers and creators of wealth is tyranny pure and simple."

Utah men were generally supportive, having previously survived seventeen years of women voting without the sky falling in. But the men's levels of enthusiasm varied, Democrats being rather more enthusiastic than Republicans and Mormons being more supportive than gentiles. The LDS Church took no official stand, and among the leadership, support was not unanimous. Angus Cannon's brother George Q. was opposed. The big concern was that putting women's suffrage in the proposed state constitution would get Utah's statehood petition a thumbs down in Washington, D.C. After all, Utah seemed strange enough as it was without joining the freak states. Braver voices included that of second counselor to the first presidency Joseph F. Smith (the nephew of church founder Joseph Smith), who would go on to become sixth president of the LDS Church, who said, "Let them who will not enter into the door of equal rights and impartial suffrage step aside, and leave the passage clear to those who desire to enter."

Using all the feminine wiles at their disposal, Mattie and her suffragist friends feted the members of the constitutional convention at a gala that featured the Ladies Mandolin and Guitar Club. Tables were set with white and purple lilacs, red tulips and roses. "Ices" were served. The *Salt Lake Herald Tribune* called it "A Brilliant Affair." Angus attended.

On July 11, 1895, Dr. Mattie Hughes Cannon "made a very able address" to the Eleventh Ward Democrats, according to the *Salt Lake Herald.* In the cerebral and idealistic vein of nineteenth-century political oratory (oh, if we could revive that!) she made common ground with everyone in attendance, praising Jeffersonian ideals, specifically the "leveling of aristocracy."

Then she stuck a dagger to the heart of the Cult of True Womanhood: "Mrs. Cannon declared she had no sympathy with the cry that politics would lead women to neglect their homes. She had seen many homes worse kept by women always in them than those of women who sometimes get out and breathe a little ozone," the *Salt Lake Herald* reported. "Too many women stay in home so much that they lose vitality and breath. A political campaign may bring out some women who have stayed in their homes too much." Then Mattie told a joke about an eagle mating with a hen and a salmon sleeping with a clam, which reportedly was an uproarious hit with the Democrats. We twenty-first centurions wouldn't get it.

THE FIRST WOMAN IN line to register to vote on August 7, 1895, was Dr. Martha Hughes Cannon. Registrar Crowley of the Second Precinct "took time by the forelock," putting women on his voting list, even though the courts had not yet decided if women would actually be able to vote in the fall election. In line right behind her was Amelia Folsom Young, a widow of Brigham Young.

"I hope the courts will decide women have not the right to vote," a prominent Republican told the *Salt Lake Herald.* Republicans were anxious, because the women "will go against us." The soon-to-be state was rife with wives and servant girls, leaving for the Republicans "that class of men who are living as bachelors and therefore cannot double their strength."

Utah women wouldn't get to vote in the 1895 election, but they won anyway.

On November 5, 1895, the Utah State Constitution was approved, with 28,618 men voting yes and 2,687 men voting no. Enshrined in it was this: "Both male and female citizens of this State shall enjoy equally all civil, political, and religious rights and privileges." Less than one hundred years later, Utah made an about-face. Even though the Equal Rights Amendment says virtually the same thing: "Equality of rights under the law shall not be denied or abridged by the United States or by any state on account of sex," Utah refused to ratify the ERA. (But the state didn't take it out of its constitution, either.)

Utah became the forty-fifth state on January 4, 1896.

Dr. Mattie Hughes Cannon wasted no time enjoying her renewed political rights.

16

ALL'S FAIR IN LOVE AND POLITICS

The 1896 Race for Utah State Senate

Balconies were festooned with bunting while clusters of small American flags were hung all around the interior of the opera house" when the Salt Lake Democrats met to nominate their candidates in September 1896. Dr. Mattie Hughes Cannon chaired the credentials committee. In local party politics, that's a powerful but thankless job. Angus had a job there, too. Never mind that he was a Republican, the Democrats made him their sergeant-at-arms.

When it came time for nominations for state senate, Mr. J.R. Letcher stood up. "Thirty-four years ago today our handsome chairman was born," he began, referring to Mattie. The crowd cheered. "Under the new condition of things in Utah, and under the new constitution the women have the right of suffrage. My candidate is the graduate of two medical colleges but yet withal a womanly woman. If nominated she will be elected and go to the legislature with the sole idea of performing her duty to her constituents.… Her name is Dr. Mattie Hughes Cannon and I dare any man to vote against her." The crowd cheered merrily.

Seven nominees competed for four slots on the Salt Lake County Democratic ticket for state senate. Dr. Mattie came out on top on the first ballot, getting 373 votes. Trailing her but still making the cut were George Whitaker (345), John Caine (322) and D.O. Rideout (248). George Romney, a distant relative of 2012 Republican presidential candidate Willard "Mitt" Romney, missed the boat entirely with a paltry 174 votes. The final Democratic slate would also include the Populist Party nominee B.A. Harbour for a total of five candidates.

Making the most of her thirty-five-dollar budget, Mattie Hughes Cannon hit the campaign circuit, shaking hands and explaining her political philosophy to anyone who would listen.

"Dr. Cannon took the women's view of the questions presented by politics and told why she is a Democrat and why other women should be Democrats," the *Salt Lake Herald* reported on her visit to the West Jordan Democrats. "She said that the Democrats were for the greatest possible liberty, while the Republicans were for restrictions. Love of liberty is inherited from our Pilgrim fathers. The speaker urged women to register and vote this fall so that their good influence might be felt immediately in our politics." It was an "enthusiastic rally." She also spoke in Brigham City, Draper, to the Scandinavian Democrats and around Salt Lake County.

The *Herald*, ever Mattie's most breathless fan, reported on her speech to the Fifteenth Ward.

> *Martha Hughes Cannon was the first to address the people in a neat speech. Beginning with the declaration that the women of Utah are Democrats, she explained the reasons. Democracy is a just cause to start with. The women of today are the daughters of the women of yesterday; those who came across the plains in '47 can trace their ancestry to the Pilgrims, who sailed the stormy Atlantic in order to found a democracy, where they might have the freedom to worship God. The sentiments which animated the breasts of the mothers of the republic have been transmitted to the children through all the succeeding generations and exist stronger than ever, fostered and encouraged under Democratic rule.*

You must admit, Mattie got her money's worth with that degree from Pennsylvania's National School of Elocution and Oratory.

The *Herald* raved some more.

> *Mrs. Cannon took up the questions of women in politics. It is said by those who oppose woman having the franchise that when she dabbles in politics, she neglects her home and family. There is no truth in that statement. The true woman cannot be induced to forget her duties by reason of political activity, any more than the true man can be influenced to fail to perform his part of the work. These points were appreciated by the audience, which applauded the speaker generously for her effort.*

Democracy, liberty and Pilgrims weren't the only things being argued about. There were also the issues of polygamy and prohibition. Mattie supported polygamy (she kind of had to) but opposed prohibition of liquor. This seems a little strange, considering that Mormons eschew alcohol and she herself had complained about her "boozer" aunt. She explained: "On the saloon question I stand with my party. Prohibition does not prohibit. So what earthly use is there of mixing things up with a party that's always preaching something that they never practice." Her words proved prophetic. She would live long enough to watch the Eighteenth Amendment turn into a disaster of bathtub gin and speakeasies.

Mattie was actually more interested in pragmatic state-level issues, such as sewage disposal and garbage pick-up. "I shall take real interest in all the sanitary bills, of course, and all bills pertaining to educational matters. Women are good ones for those things. We know how to keep house and we know how to keep a city." True that.

REPUBLICANS NOMINATED ANGUS FOR their slate of five state senate candidates in October. He had a pretty fine reputation, and all the Mormons knew him because he prayed and preached in the tabernacle all the time. Candidate Angus had a few problems, however. He had besmirched his own reputation just two months prior, when, according to the *Salt Lake Herald*, a "wordy battle" almost turned into a "fistic conflict" between him and another man over the election of an LDS bishop. The newspaper reported that Mr. Cannon had ordered a certain Mr. Harrington to "shut up and sit down." When Mr. Harrington refused, Angus "lost his equanimity and then followed a bitter colloquy, in which church decorum and priestly dignity were entirely forgotten, and in which the two gentlemen exchanged personalities in a manner that would put to shame a wrangle between curbstone politicians. Back and forth the angry words flew while the angry churchmen grew red in the face." (Why, oh why can't we enjoy such theatrical reporting nowadays?)

The police were called. Angus apologized for losing his temper, explaining that he was recovering from a severe illness.

All the jocularity over his wife running against him had to have him rankled. Even the *Salt Lake Tribune*, which would eventually endorse him, teased, "What would draw a bigger crowd, to whom the truths of Democracy might be expounded, than the prospect of a verbal set-to between Dr. Mattie Hughes Cannon and her husband, Angus M. Cannon?"

Mattie's not-so-secret weapons were women. To be fair, the Republicans nominated their own woman to their ticket, the estimable Emmeline Wells, but the Democrats were seen as being more enthusiastic about welcoming the ladies. They'd been organizing "with a vim" since 1895. Mattie had served on the Democratic Great Committee of one hundred women who were each charged with recruiting one hundred other women to form a one-thousand-woman advisory body to the state's Democratic Party. The *Salt Lake Herald* reported the women "did their work quickly and well. There was no unnecessary discussion." Anyone who has ever served on any kind of committee knows that was some kind of miracle—or fake news.

The newspapers battled over the two Cannons. Opening salvo came from the *Salt Lake Tribune* on October 30, 1896:

> *Angus M. Cannon has been a resident here almost from boyhood. He has filled many important stations and with perfect satisfaction. He knows almost every inch of Utah from personal observation; he knows the wants of the State as well as any man within its borders. He is a gentleman of superior abilities, and is an all-around clear-cut man of affairs. We know of no one who has the slightest doubt of his election.*

The *Herald* responded the next day in its charmingly snarky way:

> *Our morning contemporary says that Hon. Angus M. Cannon is a worthy man and deserving of the people's suffrages. Against him we haven't a word in the world to say, only we would say that **Mrs. Cannon, his wife, is the better man of the two.** Send Mrs. Cannon to the state senate as a Democrat and let Mr. Cannon as a Republican remain at home to manage home industry.* [Emphasis added.]

Not to be outdone, the *Tribune* snarked right back:

> *Our morning contemporary, we fear, is seeking to breed domestic troubles. We were pleased a day or two since to say a kindly word for Mr. Angus M. Cannon, Sr., and to intimate that in our judgment, in the manner of legislative business he might be even superior to Mrs. Cannon, and now the* Herald *comes out and says that Mrs. Mattie Hughes Cannon is the better man of the two. We do not see anything for Angus M. to do but to*

> *either go home and break a bouquet over Mrs. Cannon's head, to show his*
> *superiority, or to go up to the Herald office and break a chair over the head*
> *of the man who wrote that disturber of domestic peace.*

Back east, the *New York Times* somehow missed the battle. On November 1, 1896, the nation's most famous newspaper featured a nice photograph of Martha Hughes Cannon under the staidest headline imaginable: "Women Office Seekers." The *Times* praised Utah women voters for their "true independence" and Mattie for her "intense independence by declining to follow the political convictions of her husband" and then inexplicably failed to mention that her husband was running for the same position.

REPUBLICANS GOT WALLOPED IN Utah on Election Day 1896. Mattie and Angus's then-eleven-year-old daughter Lizzie remembered years later her father "sweating blood"—and rightly so. *Landslide* and *disaster* were the descriptors employed by the newspapers. The *Salt Lake Herald* summed it up: "Utah yesterday experienced a complete change of heart, politically, the silver tide carrying the state into the Democratic column with a grand rush." William Jennings Bryan took the new state's three electoral votes. All five of the candidates on the Democratic/Populist ticket for Salt Lake County state senate seats won, including Mattie Hughes Cannon, and all five Republicans lost, including Angus Cannon. Nationwide, it was a different matter. The sparsely populated states of the South and West went solidly for Bryan but were outvoted by McKinley's more populated strongholds in the Northeast and upper Midwest.

Newspapers reported that Mattie beat Angus by "a neat little majority of 4,000 votes." That was something of a tidy exaggeration. Nevertheless, there's no question she got thousands more votes than he did; it wasn't even close, and nobody was claiming the election was rigged.

It wasn't really a head-to-head race between Mattie and Angus, though. That's the way tour guides tell the story, how newspapers spun it at the time and even how short histories imply it was. The matchup was a little more complicated. The Salt Lake County Republicans nominated a slate of five candidates for state senate, and the Democrats fielded a slate of five candidates. A voter could check a single box to vote for the entire slate or mix and match votes for any five of the individuals. Theoretically, both Mattie and Angus could have won a seat. But it didn't work out that way.

Senator Cannon, front and center. *By permission, Utah State Historical Society.*

Mattie Hughes Cannon was not the only woman Utahns elected in 1896, which, don't forget, was a quarter century before women could even vote in most states. Democrats Eurithe La Barthe and Sarah Anderson won seats in the Utah State House of Representatives.

150

But it was the polygamous wife who got all the press. Her election made the papers all over the United States. Just a few that carried the story were the *Boston Daily Globe*, the *Daily Iowa Capitol*, the *Philadelphia Times* and the *Norwalk Evening Gazette*. The *Portland* (ME) *Daily Press* described Mattie as "an active woman suffragist with ultra-modern ideas" who can "whip her lord and master at the polls."

Probably the country's most famous "sob sister" (a female journalist who covered social issues), Annie Laurie of the *San Francisco Examiner* actually went to Salt Lake City to meet and interview Mattie. A hell of a reporter, Annie Laurie was, ironically, opposed to women voting, but she sure wrote a bang-up report:

> *Martha Hughes Cannon, the senator, is a doctor by profession. She lives in a neat little red brick house in a neat little three-set street. She has a little girl 11 years old and a little boy seven years old. She is between 30 and 36 to look at, and she is a clear-skinned, slender, trim little woman, well-groomed and fresh, with brown hair plentifully sprinkled with gray and a pair of brilliant, alert hazel eyes. She has little bits of thin hands and little bits of slim feet, and she wears good clothes of a quiet, unobtrusive kind. She has a clear voice and a good serviceable vocabulary, and she is perfectly free from self-consciousness of any sort.*

Looking beyond her fixation on grooming, the addition of the fact that Mattie had apparently given up on hair dye, the left-handed compliment about a "serviceable vocabulary" and the way she larded it up with all the little this and little that's (seven *littles* in one paragraph), Annie Laurie (her real name was Winifred Sweet Black) must be commended for her thorough reporting.

Mattie described Election Day for Annie Laurie's readers: "I went to the polls and voted. Then I went and attended to my patients. I beat Mr. Cannon by a majority of something like 4,000. I heard a prominent politician say that he wished Mr. Cannon and I had both been elected. He said he'd liked to have seen the fight. He would have been disappointed. If a woman quarrels over politics with her husband she'd quarrel with him over whether he liked biscuit or raised bread or any other subject that came in handy."

Of course, Annie Laurie had to ask about polygamy. Her readers would want to know. Dr. Mattie was forthright about it:

> *"I believe in polygamy....Of course the law of the land says 'no,' and we must obey. But that does not alter one's belief in the right of the thing."* She

Sob sister Annie
Laurie opposed
women's suffrage.
*Library of Congress,
LC-USZ62-97199.*

went on to describe its advantages, specifically the freedom. "[A plural
wife] *and her children order their lives, and do not have to wait and be
ready for her husband….A plural wife has more time to herself and more
independence every way than a single one….That is not the reason I believe
in it. I believe in it because it is right. Jealousy, unhappiness? Not half as
much of it among plural wives as there is among single wives."*

Mattie was shining the best light on the situation for the reading public.
She was, in fact, jealous, and Angus, at the time, was apparently giving her
far more "freedom" than she appreciated having. Eating vinegar with a fork,
as she was wont to do, that same year, Mattie invited her husband to dinner
via a note that read: "If you would care to come. I would not for the world
interfere with anybody's day, however. We modern polygs are learning our

station." But she was not about to air that kind of disillusionment to the readers of the *San Francisco Examiner.*

Then Mattie stuck it to the antisuffragist sob sister interviewing her. "Sixty percent of the voters of this state are women. Did you realize that? Oh, we control the state. Intelligent women we are, too, the Mormon women."

Of course, Mattie was asked to defend her mothering, just as working moms still have to do today, over a century later. She was no helicopter parent, that's for sure.

> *What am I going to do with my children while I am making laws for the state? The same thing I have done with them when I have been practicing medicine. They have been left to themselves a good deal, and I must say they compare very favorably with children who need a governess and a nurse and a mamma to look after them every minute. Somehow I know that women who stay at home all the time have the most unpleasant homes there are. You give me a woman who thinks about something besides cook stoves and wash tubs and baby flannels, and I'll show you, nine times out of ten, a successful mother.*

Then Mattie shared her remarkably modern take on gendered behavior: "I can't bear a mannish woman or a mannish man either. By mannish I mean, you perceive, not an inherent quality, but an assumption, a sticking out of the elbows and a raising of the head and a strutting." Mattie pantomimed for Annie Laurie before continuing. "That is as offensive to me in a man as in a woman. All the best men I know are ladylike and all the best women I know are gentlemanly. You catch my idea, I perceive."

Well, Annie Laurie admitted she most definitely did not catch the idea, but we of the twenty-first century are, maybe, finally starting to perceive what Dr. Mattie meant.

17

A BIG BATTLE, BILLS
AND BABY BROUHAHA

Senator Mattie Goes to the Capitols

Utahns bestowed bipartisan best wishes on Senator Martha Hughes Cannon and the other newly elected women. Emmeline Wells, who had run on the losing Republican slate, magnanimously extolled the virtues of Mattie and the Democratic winners on the pages of her *Woman's Exponent*. "These are all women in the prime of life, with good mentality and manifest activity, and capability in other positions, and it seems a foregone conclusion that they will acquit themselves well and do honor to the cause of equal suffrage."

The Republican-leaning *Salt Lake Tribune*, the same paper that had instructed Angus to "break a bouquet over Mrs. Cannon's head," described the new senator as "a brilliant and accomplished lady, and a forcible and eloquent speaker." It described Representative Sarah Anderson as "remarkably well posted on matters of current interest" with "well-formed and positive opinions." Representative Eurithe La Barthe was "well-educated and a recognized leader in educational and local matters."

Nationwide, the public was more skeptical. How could it possibly work to have women mixing it up with men in the dirty business of politics? The *Philadelphia Record* fretted over how things could possibly get "thrashed out" in the presence of women, because "a resort to rudeness is an indispensable condition of fruitful debate." *Pshaw*, responded the *Salt Lake Herald*, "The presence of women in the legislature will be not to prevent all legislators saying what they wish to, but to compel them to say it in better style."

MATTIE'S BETTER STYLE SHONE in the first big battle of the newly elected Utah state legislature: picking a U.S. senator. (A civic factoid all Americans should know but hardly anybody does is that until the Seventeenth Amendment was passed in 1913, U.S. senators were chosen by state legislatures, not voters.) Bucking both her church and her husband's family, in 1897 Mattie stood up to use her considerable oratorical skills to make her pitch for Moses Thatcher for the U.S. Senate (over Joseph Rawlins, Henry Henderson and Edward Critchlow).

Thatcher was on the outs with the LDS Church and a bitter enemy of Mattie's brother-in-law George Q. Cannon, but those things didn't hold a bit of sway with Senator Mattie, who proclaimed:

> *The great statesman that I shall vote for today will be an honor to his country; he will serve the varied interests of our young State well, and last but not least, he will do your church nor my church no wrong, for in his heart there is no bitterness. His honor is as bright as the sunlight that flashes on the snow-capped crest of great Nebo, and his life is as pure as the limpid waters that leap from our mountain crags. Mr. President, I this day cast my ballot for the greatest Roman of them all, the Honorable Moses Thatcher.*

"Tremendous applause" followed. Senator Mattie's picture was featured in both the *Herald* and the *Tribune*. Representative Cook of Rich County was

Utah's state legislature met here until the capitol was built. *Getty Museum.*

so impressed he decided that Mattie, not Moses, was actually the "greatest Roman of them all" (Roman being a nickname for senators) and voted for her instead. His endorsement of Mattie got a "decorous murmur of applause."

To thank Senator Cannon for her support, Thatcher gave her a handsome bouquet of roses. With a feminist flourish and extravagant egalitarianism, she separated the flowers into individual stems and doled them out to her brother senators.

Neither of the two "greatest Romans" went on to win. After endless rounds of balloting, Democrat Joseph Rawlins managed to pull together enough votes to go to Washington. All the women stuck with Moses Thatcher to the bitter end. Moses came in second with twenty-nine votes. Mattie got four.

EDUCATION AND HEALTH WERE the top issues for 1890s legislators. Then there was the super-pressing controversy over "high hats." Representative Eurithe La Barthe introduced a bill to require women to remove their towering millinery of feathers and frou-frous when entering a theater. Her peers derided her bill as trivial. But was it? When you pay good money for tickets to *The Importance of Being Earnest* (the 1895 Oscar Wilde play that is still performed today), who wants to duck and weave to see the performance through and over the "waving plumes and nodding garden flowers" of some show-off fashionista? Look at photographs of Victorian headgear. Give Eurithe a break. She was a problem-solver.

Mattie, for her part, introduced three bills: an Act to Protect the Health of Women and Girl Employees; an Act Providing for the Compulsory Education of Deaf, Dumb and Blind Children; and an Act Creating a State Board of Health. She supported pure food and drug initiatives and fought against the effort to abolish certifications for doctors and midwives. She didn't want quacks practicing medicine in Utah.

Her Act to Protect the Health of Women and Girl Employees was straightforward. Shop and factory owners had to provide women and girls with chairs. This seems reasonable enough, but business owners argued that since their male employees stood all day, so should the ladies. Never mind that men could wear comfy flat shoes while ladies had to stand in pinchy heels.

Governor Wells appointed Mattie to the Board of Public Health in 1898. The board worked on regulations to disinfect and restrict the transportation of sick livestock. They figured out how to improve the accuracy of vital statistics, suggested improvements to septic systems and the water supply and set up licensure for embalmers. They drafted quarantine protocols for infectious diseases and established rules to keep unvaccinated children out of school during smallpox epidemics. The latter was in response to antivaxxer misinformation published by the *Deseret News*, which claimed vaccines were unsafe. History does repeat itself, doesn't it?

"IT'S GOING GREAT" WAS the message Senator Martha Hughes Cannon took to the United States Congress in 1898 about the "experiment" in women's suffrage taking place in the freak states of Utah, Colorado, Wyoming and Idaho. She stopped off in Washington after speaking at the National American Woman Suffrage Association's thirtieth annual convention.

"There is strong and cumulative evidence that even those who opposed equal suffrage with the greatest ability and vehemence would not now vote to repeal the measure," she told the men in Washington, D.C. "None of the unpleasant results which were predicted have occurred."

She scoffed at the True Woman advocates. "The contentions in families, tarnishment of woman's charm, the destruction of ideals, have been found to be ghosts of unfounded prejudice," she testified. And surely, if anyone could provide firsthand evidence that women's suffrage did not cause "contentions in families," it's the wife and mother who beat her own husband in an election.

Mattie and others lobbied Congress for women's suffrage. *Library of Congress, LC-DIG-ppmsca-58145.*

The *Chicago Record* was impressed. "Mrs. Dr. Martha Hughes Cannon… is considered one of the brightest exponents of the women's cause in the United States."

Seconding her comments to Congress was Mormon women's most famous feminist friend, Susan B. Anthony, plus State Representative Martha Bushnell Conine of Colorado. But a fat lot of good that did. It would be another twenty-two years before most of the rest of the United States stopped denying women the right to vote.

THE STORK DELIVERED BIG trouble in an itty-bitty bundle in 1899, the third year of Senator Cannon's term. "Senator Martha Hughes Cannon's Baby!" trumpeted the *Ogden Daily Standard* on April 22, 1899. "Dr. Martha Hughes Cannon is gaining as much notoriety over giving birth to a baby girl as is accorded an Empress or Queen when an heir to the throne is born," the *Standard* continued. "The arrival of the little stranger at the Cannon home in Salt Lake has been telegraphed far and wide."

Baby Gwendolyn had arrived on April 17, 1899. She joined big sister Elizabeth and big brother James.

Into this happy milieu marched a newcomer to Utah, described by the *Salt Lake Herald* as a "somewhat erratic and anti-Mormon fanatic." He was also a stringer for the *New York Journal.* In July 1899, Charles Mostyn Owen took it upon himself to swear out a complaint against Angus Cannon for polygamy, using Gwendolyn's birth as his evidence. The sheriff didn't have any excuse to avoid it, so he sent out his deputy to arrest Angus. Luckily, Angus's son John M. Cannon was a lawyer and quickly bonded out his dad. The *Salt Lake Tribune* caught up with Angus at the LDS tithing office, where Angus was "perspiring freely and looked sorely troubled."

For her part, Mattie was neither perspiring nor troubled. The same *Tribune* found her "attired in a rose-colored tea gown trimmed in cream lace and appeared to be enjoying the best of health." She refused to discuss the case with the *Tribune* reporter but was gracious enough and "chatted pleasantly for some time on various other topics of general interest." For her friends at the *Herald*, she did one better. Still refusing to discuss Angus's arrest, she "delightedly exhibited the 10 weeks' old baby, which, as she says, has 'raised all the rumpus.' And the mother, as she dangled the small bundle, insisted that she must not worry over the result of the new fight, because she had to get strong and well to take her baby away from the hot weather and the city."

Senator Cannon and the baby who raised all the rumpus. *By permission, Utah State Historical Society.*

Meanwhile, "Mormon Baby May Convict Cannon" screamed the headline on the top of the front page of the July 9, 1899 *New York Journal*, illustrated with large photographs of both Angus and Mattie. The *Journal* tracked the case in far-off Utah closely, following up with an article titled "The Defiant Polygamist." Reading past the splashy headlines, it's clear Angus and Mattie were mere proxies for the real target of the New York rag's yellow journalism— Brigham H. Roberts. Spotlighting the Cannons and their baby girl was meant to embarrass Roberts, the Mormon polygamist who had been elected to the U.S. House of Representatives. The *Journal* was handing ammunition to Roberts's opponents. The House never seated Roberts.

Back in Utah, how was Angus to get out of his pickle? There was no chance he would deny Gwendolyn's paternity. Some speculated he might argue that Mattie, not his first wife, Sarah, was his true wife. Legally, this would have made a slick defense, since under a court decision, each polygamist was permitted to select any one of his wives to be his legal wife.

Nine years had already passed since the manifesto allegedly ended polygamy in Utah, but there had never been a consensus on what, precisely, had ended. LDS president Woodruff had made it clear that further polygamous marriages would not be performed in the United States under his watch, but what about current polygamous wives? Anti-Mormons insisted each husband should pick one wife and leave the others be, but polygamous husbands interpreted things differently. Brigham Young's son told an audience in Chicago that he'd be a "scoundrel" to abandon any of his wives but assured them the practice would soon die out since the polygamists were "old men" who would "soon pass away." All most polygamists agreed to do was be satisfied with the wives they already had and act discreetly in public.

Regardless of the unsettled status of polygamy, Utah Mormons and non-Mormons alike were sick of the entire controversy and weren't happy that this zealot Charles Mostyn Owen was stirring up the hornet's nest all over again. Coverage in the *Deseret News* was subdued, with short articles under boring headlines like "Mr. Cannon in Logan" and "Angus M. Cannon Appears in Court." Articles in Utah's gentile press were splashier but treated the Cannons with more respect than opprobrium.

Meanwhile, the sheriff's deputies raced about town, serving subpoenas. Mattie, being busy with her patients, was hard to pin down. According to the *Herald*, it took the deputy three attempts to find her. "I expected you," she said, when he finally handed over the subpoena. Cannon's first wife, Sarah Cannon, was easier to locate but told the deputy, "Well, I don't have to say anything and I shall not do so." The man who delivered baby Gwendolyn, Dr. Bascom, "threw up his hands in evidence of disgust when the summons was handed to him."

None of the subpoenaed witnesses had to testify. Standing up with his attorney son, Angus pleaded guilty. The judge noted that the complaining party, Mr. Owen, had not shown any damages, and neither Mattie nor Sarah (the named wives) claimed injury. "It seems to me that a light fine will answer the demands of justice," he said, ordering Angus to pay a $100 fine. The whole shebang lasted all of two weeks.

Charles Owen was disappointed, to say the least. He'd been planning on filing an entire slew of cases against other polygamists. Angus's light fine dampened his "enthuzimuzzy" (that's Victorian for enthusiasm) considerably. He moved to Nevada.

Mattie did not run for reelection when her term expired in 1900.

18

TWENTIETH-CENTURY CODA

After Two Steps Forward, It's One Step Back

How soon we forget. Less than a decade after she left office, Senator Martha Hughes Cannon was already receding into distant memory. In 1908, the *Salt Lake Herald* ran a "Remember When" column about the remarkable 1896 election that had already been forgotten. In 1911, the *Salt Lake Tribune* got miffed when Coloradans claimed its legislators were the first to cast votes for a woman to the U.S. Senate. (Remember Representative Cook and the three others who voted for Mattie, the "greatest Roman of them all," for U.S. Senate in 1897.) In 1913, the *Ogden Daily Standard* had to set the record straight when others reported that Colorado's Helen Ring Robinson was the country's first woman state senator.

Enthusiasm for electing women legislators waned considerably after the turn of the century. The *Woman's Exponent* rued the fact that so few women were being nominated for elected office: "It proves how strongly the old traditions and prejudices are against women in public life." Inside and outside the freak states, women continued to march for a constitutional amendment giving all adult U.S. women the right to vote, but few ran for office.

Angus suffered a string of bad luck in the new century. In 1900, a horse crushed his leg. Then in 1904, he was forced to traipse to Washington, D.C., to testify against his fellow Mormon, Senator Reed Smoot. Angus was asked about his own polygamy, prosecutions and stint in prison and responded in a voice "quivering with ill-suppressed emotion." Angus fell ill after his second wife and supposed favorite, Amanda, died in 1905. Two years later, he suffered a stroke but recovered. In 1915, he gave up the ghost for good. He was eighty-one.

Senator Cannon served long before most women could even vote. *Library of Congress, LC-DIG-ppmsca-56874.*

Mattie continued to practice medicine and raise her children. She stayed active in politics and public service but never ran for office again. She delivered a series of lectures on "Woman in Politics" in 1900. She remained on the Board of Health and was a delegate to the Democratic State Convention more than once. She was appointed to the Medico-Legal Society of New York and was active in the American Congress of Tuberculosis.

In 1906, she spoke at a celebration of Thomas Jefferson's birthday. Her name and stature continued to be associated with the fight for female suffrage. In 1908, she got short mentions in both the *Philadelphia Record* and *Bay City* (**MI**) *Times*. Ever her biggest fan, the *Salt Lake Herald* showcased Mattie in a long, multipage feature story headlined "Progress of Utah Women Shows Complete Success of Women Suffrage" in 1910, which was still ten years before most women in the United States could vote. Illustrated with large photographs of four prestigious Utah women, Mattie's photograph was the

The Nineteenth Amendment gave all American women the vote in 1920. *Library of Congress, LC-DIG-npcc-29566.*

largest. In 1916, she went on a 1,300-mile and thirteen-stop speaking tour. The headline in the *Salt Lake Telegram* was "She's Not Superstitious."

After the decades-long fight for women's suffrage was finally won with passage of the Nineteenth Amendment, Mattie didn't rest. In 1922, she helped raise $500,000 for war orphans in Europe.

By this time, she was splitting her time between Utah and California. She spent time in Pacific Grove, San Diego and Los Angeles.

All three of her children, Lizzie, James and Gwendolyn, married monogamously. James founded Cannon Electric Company in California, supplying equipment to Hollywood movie producers, alarms for businesses and electrical parts for World War II aircraft.

Gwendolyn, the daughter whose 1899 birth "raised all the rumpus," grew up to be a spunky '20s flapper, tarted up with long beaded necklaces and a hairdo of ringlets. She died of tuberculosis in 1928. Her mother was crushed.

Mattie was diagnosed with cancer in 1931. She died on July 10, 1932, aged seventy-five, in Los Angeles, survived by her daughter Elizabeth; son, James; and six grandchildren. Her funeral was held in Salt Lake City. She was buried in the Salt Lake City Cemetery alongside Angus and his other five wives, all lined up like matches in a matchbook.

THE MARCH OF PROGRESS is so much gammon and spinach. (That means nonsense. One must never miss an opportunity to utilize Victorian slang!)

Progress doesn't march, it dances. At best, it takes two steps forward, one step back. Sometimes, it leaps forward, sometimes backward and, other times, it sashays side to side. It most definitely does not march. The nineteenth-century Mormons reached back thousands of years to the biblical patriarchs to resurrect the practice of plural wives. And then, that same ancient practice propelled them to become among the most feminist and progressive groups of their century. Once they abandoned the practice (sort of), they worked super hard to blend into the "modern" United States, which, for them, meant stepping back from progressivism.

In 1900, the women of Utah gifted Susan B. Anthony with a bolt of silk in honor of her eightieth birthday. Anthony thanked them with these words: "The fact that the mulberry trees grew in Utah, that the silk worms made their cocoons there, that women reeled and spun and colored and wove the silk in a free State, greatly enhances its value."

Soon thereafter, the Mormon and feminist *Woman's Exponent* moderated its zeal for working women and female industrial enterprise. The feminist ideals of Second President Brigham Young and Sixth President Joseph F. Smith (the champion of equal pay for equal work) were tucked away. Even before Senator Mattie Hughes Cannon died, the *Deseret News* quoted a sermon by J. Reuben Clark, who complained that women of the past had been wrong to place themselves in competition with men.

At the onset of World War II, the LDS Church even counseled women against answering their country's urgent call to work in war industries. Rather than become Rosie the Riveters, Mormon women were urged to plant victory gardens and can beans. From then until 1989, the church encouraged women to work outside the home only when there was "true need," such as divorce, widowhood or the long-term disability of her husband. As late as 1983, LDS president Gordon Hinckley insisted that "man is the provider," although he reversed this opinion just six years later, resurrecting the almost-forgotten sentiments of his long-ago predecessor

Brigham Young. In 1989, Hinkley urged Mormon women to "get all the education you can. Train yourself to make a contribution to the society in which you live.…Almost the entire field of human endeavor is now open to women."

The Cult of True Womanhood has morphed into not much more than a font of silly jokes for docents at Victorian house museums. The only vestige taken seriously by anyone is the "separate spheres" argument still held dear by evangelicals, fundamentalists and, ironically, some Mormons. No one is seriously lobbying to take away women's right to vote in secular elections, but the "separate spheres" rationalization lives on in refusals to let women preach or hold leadership positions in churches. Virtually all mainline Christian denominations ordain women. But Roman Catholics, Mormons, fundamentalists and most evangelicals do not.

The LDS Church became an outspoken opponent of the Equal Rights Amendment in the 1970s and 1980s, even though the ERA is practically plagiarized from the Utah Constitution their ancestors drafted the century before. In 2019, an LDS spokesman proclaimed, "The church's position on this issue has been consistent for more than forty years." That's true enough, but it is inconsistent with LDS views from 140 years ago.

Today's mainline LDS Church is vehemently antipolygamy. History can be an embarrassment. The Oneida stainless flatware manufacturers literally tried to burn their entire "free love commune" backstory (they had a documents bonfire). Today's Saints aren't lighting bonfires, but they would prefer we quit smirking about their past as well. As Kimball Young wrote in 1954, "The system was all right at the time, but they hoped it would never be reinstated." The revulsion against it is so strong that in the 2018 BBC documentary *Three Wives*, plural widows couldn't buy a headstone for their deceased husband in Utah. They had to go to Colorado to find an engraver willing to put all their names on it.

Today's law enforcement does not prosecute polygamy absent another violation, such as welfare fraud, underage marriage or abuse. But it's grounds for excommunication from the LDS Church. Practitioners of plural marriage belong to break-away sects, of which there are too many to count. Jon Krakauer in *Under the Banner of Heaven* estimated there are two hundred polygamous Mormon sects. Some plural wives are instantly recognizable by their disturbing youth, pastel prairie dresses and elaborate hairdos. (The polygamists' prairie dresses were actually a 1980s innovation.) Plural wives in more progressive sects marry late, work outside the home and dress to blend into any crowd of twenty-first-century women.

But even the most "modern" plural wives can't hold a candle to Senator Dr. Martha Hughes Cannon. The *Three Wives* documentary follows a pretty-much-modern polygamous family in Utah. In one scene, the wives accompany their husband to the capitol in Salt Lake City to hear him speak *on their behalf* at a rally. Mattie would never have allowed Angus to speak *on her behalf*. Had he ever the audacity to try, she would have beaten him to the lectern.

Today, the Utah Department of Health works out of the Martha Hughes Cannon Health Building in Salt Lake City. A statue of her was placed in the Utah Capitol Rotunda in 1996. The University of Utah produced a biopic of her life in 2012. And yet, for all that, her incredible story—"Polygamous Wife #4 Beats Her Own Husband to Become First Female Senator in the United States"—remains nearly impossible to believe and is mostly unknown.

But it's true.

BIBLIOGRAPHY

When you take stuff from one writer it's plagiarism,
when you take from many writers it's research.
—Wilson Mizner (1933), plagiarizing Professor Notestein of Yale (1929)

Academic Journals

Alexander, Thomas G. "An Experiment in Progressive Legislation. The Granting of Woman Suffrage in Utah in 1870." First printed in 1970. In *Battle for the Ballot.* Edited by Carol Cornwall Madsen. Logan: Utah State University Press, 1997.

Beecher, Maureen Ursenbach. "The 'Leading Sisters': A Female Hierarchy in Nineteenth-Century Mormon Society." *Journal of Mormon History* 9 (1982): 25–39.

Beecher, Maureen Ursenbach, Carol Cornwall Madsen and Jill Mulvay Derr. "The Latter-Day Saints and Women's Rights, 1970–1920." First printed in 1979. In *Battle for the Ballot.* Edited by Carol Cornwall Madsen. Logan: Utah State University Press, 1997.

Beeton, Beverly. "Woman Suffrage in Territorial Utah." First printed in 1978. In *Battle for the Ballot.* Edited by Carol Cornwall Madsen. Logan: Utah State University Press, 1997.

Cooks, Catherine. "Rethinking Sexuality in the Progressive Era." *Journal of the Gilded Age and Progressive Era* 5, no. 2 (April 2006): 93–118.

Derr, Jill Mulvay. "Eliza R. Snow and the Woman Question." First printed in 1976. In *Battle for the Ballot.* Edited by Carol Cornwall Madsen. Logan: Utah State University Press, 1997.

———. "Woman's Place in Brigham Young's World." *Brigham Young University Studies* 18, no. 3 (Spring 1978): 377–95.

Eliason, Eric. "Curious Gentiles and Representational Authority in the City of Saints." *Religion and American Culture: A Journal of Interpretation* 11, no. 2 (Summer 2001): 155–90.

Evans, Vella Neil. "Mormon Women and the Right to Wage Work." *Dialogue: A Journal of Mormon Thought* 23, no. 4 (Winter 1990): 45–61.

Freedman, Estelle. "Sexuality in Nineteenth-Century America: Behavior, Ideology, and Politics." *Reviews in American History* 10, no. 4 (December 1982): 196–215.

Goldman, Mimi. "Prostitution in America." *Crime and Social Justice* 2 (Fall–Winter 1974): 90–93.

Groneman, Carol. "Nymphomania: The Historical Construction of Female Sexuality." *Signs* 19, no. 2 (Winter 1994): 337–67.

Haggard, Kathleen C. "In Union Is Strength: Mormon Women and Cooperation, 1867–1900." Master's thesis, Utah State University, 1998. https://digitalcommons.usu.edu/gradreports/738/.

Hall, Donald E. "Teaching Victorian Pornography: Hermeneutics and Sexuality." *Victorian Review* 34, no. 2 (Fall 2008): 19–25.

Harrison, Brian. "Underneath the Victorians." *Victorian Studies* 10, no. 3 (March 1967): 239–69.

Harvey, Karen. "The Century of Sex? Gender, Bodies, and Sexuality in the Long Eighteenth Century." *Historical Journal* 45, no. 4 (December 2002): 899–916.

Iversen, Joan. "Feminist Implications in Mormon Polygyny." *Feminist Studies* 10, no. 3 (Autumn 1984): 505–22.

———. "The Mormon Suffrage Relationship: Personal and Political Quandries." First printed in 1990. In *Battle for the Ballot.* Edited by Carol Cornwall Madsen. Logan: Utah State University Press, 1997.

Landale, Nancy S., and Avery M. Guest. "Ideology and Sexuality Among Victorian Women." *Social Science History* 10, no. 2 (Summer 1986): 147–70.

Madsen, Carol Cornwall, ed. "Schism in the Sisterhood." First printed in 1987. In *Battle for the Ballot.* Logan: Utah State University Press, 1997.

Madsen, Carol Cornwall, and David J. Whittaker. "History's Sequel: A Source Essay on Women in Mormon History." *Journal of Mormon History* 6 (1979): 123–45.

Moehling, Carolyn M., Gregory T. Niemesh and Melissa A. Thomasson. "Shut Down and Shut Out: Women Physicians in the Era of Medical Education Reform." April 2019. https://ostromworkshop.indiana.edu/pdf/piep2019/moehling-niemesh-thomasson.pdf.

Morantz, Regina Markell. "Review: Women in the Medical Profession." *Reviews in American History* 6, no. 2 (June 1978): 163–70.

Mulvay, Jill C. "Eliza R. Snow and the Woman Question." *Brigham Young University Studies* 16, no. 2 (Winter 1976): 250–64.

Nichols, Jeffrey D. "Polygamy and Prostitution: Comparative Morality in Salt Lake City, 1847–1911." *Mormon History* 27, no. 2 (Fall 2001): 1–39.

Poll, Richard D. "The Legislative Antipolygamy Campaign." *Brigham Young University Studies* 26, no. 4 (Fall 1986): 107–21.

Robertson, Stephen. "Age of Consent Laws." Children and Youth in History. https://chnm.gmu.edu/cyh/teaching-modules/230.

Sears, Hal D. "The Sex Radicals in High Victorian America." *Virginia Quarterly Review* 48, no. 3 (Summer 1972): 377–92.

Seidman, Steven. "The Power of Desire and the Danger of Pleasure: Victorian Sexuality Reconsidered." *Journal of Social History* 24, no. 1 (Autumn 1990): 47–67.

———. "Sexual Attitudes of Victorian and Post-Victorian Women." *Journal of American Studies* 23, no. 1 (April 1989): 68–72.

Simpson, Thomas W. "Mormons Study 'Abroad': Brigham Young's Romance with American Higher Education, 1867–1877." *Church History* 76, no. 4 (December 2007): 778–98.

Swedin, Eric. "'One Flesh': A Historical Overview of Latter-Day Saint Sexuality and Psychology." *Dialogue: A Journal of Mormon Thought* 31, no. 4 (Winter 1998): 1–29.

Tromp Marlene. "Spirited Sexuality: Sex, Marriage, and Victorian Spiritualism." *Victorian Literature and Culture* 31, no. 1 (2003): 67–81.

Valverde, Mariana. "The Love of Finery: Fashion and the Fallen Woman in Nineteenth-Century Social Discourse." *Victorian Studies* 32, no. 2 (Winter 1989): 168–88.

Van Wagoner, Richard S. "Mormon Polyandry in Nauvoo." *Journal of Mormon Thought* 18 (Fall 1985): 67–83. https://www.dialoguejournal.com/wp-content/uploads/sbi/articles/Dialogue_V18N03_69.pdf.

Wagenen, Lola Van. "In Their Own Behalf." First printed in 1991. In *Battle for the Ballot*. Edited by Carol Cornwall Madsen. Logan: Utah State University Press, 1997.

White, Jean Bickmore. "Gentle Persuaders: Utah's First Women Legislators." First printed in 1970. In *Battle for the Ballot*. Edited by Carol Cornwall Madsen. Logan: Utah State University Press, 1997.

Whittaker, David J. "The Bone in the Throat: Orson Pratt and the Public Announcement of Plural Marriage." *Western Historical Quarterly* 18, no. 3 (July 1987): 293–314.

———. "Early Mormon Polygamy Defenses." *Journal of Mormon History* 11 (1984): 43–63.

Books

Anderson, Patricia. *When Passion Reigned: Sex and the Victorians*. New York: Basic Books, 1995.

Bartholomew, Rebecca. *Audacious Women: Early British Mormon Immigrants*. Salt Lake City, UT: Signature Books, 1995.

Bennon, Janet, and Lisa Fishbayne Joffe. *The Polygamy Question*. Logan: Utah State University Press, 2016.

Bradley, Martha Sonntag. *Pedestals & Podiums*. Salt Lake City, UT: Signature Books, 2005.

Bushman, Claudia C., ed. *Mormon Sisters*. Logan: Utah State University Press, 1997.

Campbell, Olivia. *Women in White Coats*. New York: Park Row Books, 2021.

Coontz, Stephanie. *Marriage, A History*. New York: Viking Press, 2005.

D'Emilio, John, and Estelle B. Freedman. *Intimate Matters*. Chicago: University of Chicago Press, 1988.

Fogarty, Robert S. *All Things New: American Communes and Utopian Movements, 1860–1914*. Chicago: University of Chicago Press, 1990.

Foster, Craig L., and Marianne T. Watson. *American Polygamy: A History of Fundamentalist Mormon Faith*. Charleston, SC: The History Press, 2019.

Grana, Mari. *Pioneer, Polygamist, Politician: The Life of Dr. Martha Hughes Cannon*. Helena, MT: Two Dot, 2009.

Herman, Eleanor. *Sex with Presidents.* New York: William Morrow, 2020.

Holloran, Peter C. *Boston's Wayward Children.* Plainsboro Township, NJ: Associated University Presses, 1989.

Holloway, Mark. *Utopian Communities in America, 1680–1880.* Mineola, NY: Dover Publications, 1966.

Holt, Marilyn Irvin. *The Orphan Trains.* Lincoln: University of Nebraska Press, 1992.

Jennings, Chris. *Paradise Now: The Story of American Utopianism.* New York: Random House, 2016.

Katz, Michael B. *In the Shadow of the Poorhouse.* New York: Basic Books, 1996.

Knudsen, Shirley R. *Watonwan County History.* Raleigh, NC: Curtis Media, 1995.

Krakauer, Jon. *Under the Banner of Heaven.* New York: Doubleday, 2003.

Lauer, Robert H., and Jeanette C. Lauer. *The Spirit and the Flesh: Sex in Utopian Communities.* Lanham, MD: Scarecrow Press, 1983.

Madsen, Carol Cornwall, ed. *Battle for the Ballot.* Logan: Utah State University Press, 1997.

McLoughlin, William G. *Revivals, Awakenings, and Reform.* Chicago: University of Chicago Press, 1978.

Neilson, Reid L. *Exhibiting Mormonism: The Latter-day Saints and the 1893 World's Fair.* Oxford, UK: Oxford University Press, 2011.

Nichols, Jeffrey. *Prostitution, Polygamy and Power.* Champaign: University of Illinois Press, 2008.

Oneill, Therese. *Unmentionable.* Boston: Back Bay Books, 2016.

Pitzer, Donald E., ed. *America's Communal Utopias.* Chapel Hill: University of North Carolina Press, 1997.

Van Wagoner, Richard S. *Mormon Polygamy: A History.* 2nd ed. Salt Lake City, UT: Signature Books, 1989.

Walsh, Mary Roth. *Doctors Wanted: No Women Need Apply.* New Haven, CT: Yale University Press, 1977.

Wayland-Smith, Ellen. *Oneida: From Free Love Utopia to the Well-Set Table.* London: Picador, 2016.

Young, Kimball. *Isn't One Wife Enough?* Westport, CT: Greenwood Press, 1954.

Documentaries

Dretzin, Rachel, and Grace McNally, dir. *Keep Sweet: Pray and Obey.* Brooklyn, NY: Ark Media and Participant, 2022.

Gibbons, Tim, and Adam Hirsch, dir. *Sister Wives.* Salt Lake City, UT: Puddle Monkey Productions and Figure 8 Films, 2010.

Green, Nancy, prod. *Martha Hughes Cannon.* Salt Lake City: KUED and the University of Utah, 2012.

Lomax, Becky, Jack Warrender and Tanya Winston. *Three Wives. One Husband.* London: KEO Films and Complete Camera Company, 2014–17.

Measom, Tyler, and Jennilyn Merten, dir. *Sons of Perdition.* London: BBC, 2010.

Palmer, Maureen, and Helen Slinger, prod. *Leaving Bountiful*. Vancouver, CA: Bountiful Films Inc., 2002.

Whitney, Helen, dir. *The Mormons*. Arlington, VA: PBS, 2007.

Historic Writings

Anthony, Susan B. "Social Purity." 1895. https://susanbanthonyhouse.org/blog/wp-content/uploads/2017/07/Susan-B-Anthony-1895.pdf.

Burton, Richard F. *The City of the Saints*. 1861. Reprint, Boulder: University of Colorado Press, 1990.

Cannon, Martha Hughes. "Woman Suffrage in Utah." Testimony before the U.S. House Judiciary Committee. February 15, 1898. https://www.sendmartha.com/martha-on-suffrage.

Dickens, Charles. *The Uncommercial Traveler*. 1860. Reprint, Oxford, UK: Oxford University Press, 1958.

Froiseth, Jennie Anderson. *The Women of Mormonism*. Detroit, MI: C.G.G. Paine, 1887.

Gregory, Samuel. "Letter to Ladies, in Favor of Female Physicians for Their Own Sex." 1856. https://collections.nlm.nih.gov/catalog/nlm:nlmuid-101183079-bk.

Jacob, Udney Hay. "The Peace Maker." 1842. https://www.2bc.info/pdf/PeaceMaker.pdf.

Lieber, Constance L., and John Sillito, eds. *Letters from Exile: The Correspondence of Martha Hughes Cannon and Angus M. Cannon 1886–1888*. Salt Lake City, UT: Signature Books, 1989.

Twain, Mark. *Roughing It*. Hartford, CT: American Publishing Company 1872. (Kindle access.)

Wells, Emmeline B. "The History of Woman Suffrage in Utah 1870–1900." First printed in 1902. In *Battle for the Ballot*. Edited by Carol Cornwall Madsen. Logan: Utah State University Press, 1997.

Young, Brigham. "Discourse: An Address to the Female Relief Society." First Fifty Years of Relief Society. February 4, 1869. https://www.churchhistorianspress.org/the-first-fifty-years-of-relief-society/part-3/3-11?lang=eng.

Historic Journalism

Altoona Tribune. "This Morning's Comment." September 1, 1944.

Boston Daily Globe. February 16, 1898.

———. "Good Stories for All…She Believes in Polygamy." November 21, 1896.

Daily Iowa Capitol. "The First Woman Senator." November 20, 1896.

Deseret Evening News. Various. 1868–1907.

Deseret News. Various. 1868–1907.

Deseret Weekly. Various. 1868–1907.

Hartt, Rollin Lynde. "The Mormons." *Atlantic Monthly*, February 1900. https://www.theatlantic.com/magazine/archive/1900/02/the-mormons/305339/.

Intermountain Republican. Various. 1908.

Los Angeles Herald. March 7, 1897.

Ludlow, Fitz-Hugh. "Among the Mormons." *Atlantic*, April 1864. https://www.theatlantic.com/magazine/archive/1864/04/among-the-mormons/306013/.

New York Journal. Various. July 1899.

New York Times. "Women Office Seekers." November 1, 1896.

Ogden Daily Standard. Various. 1899–1913.

Philadelphia Times. "The First Woman Senator." November 16, 1896.

Portland (ME) *Daily Press*. "Woman in the Senate." November 21, 1896.

Provo Daily Enquirer. "Great Boon." September 24, 1896.

Salt Lake Democrat. Various. 1886.

Salt Lake Herald. Various. 1886–1913.

Salt Lake Telegram. Various. 1916.

Salt Lake Times. "The Scarlet Women." September 17, 1892.

Salt Lake Tribune. Various. 1896–1916.

Woman's Exponent. Various. 1873–1899.

Modern Media

Ballard, Jamie. "Nearly Half of Women Prefer Being Treated by a Female Doctor." YouGovAmerica. August 21, 2018. https://today.yougov.com/topics/health/articles-reports/2018/08/21/women-prefer-female-doctor.

Bates, Victoria. "The Legacy of 1885: Girls and Age of Sexual Consent." *History and Policy*, September 8, 2015. https://www.historyandpolicy.org/policy-papers/papers/the-legacy-of-1885-girls-and-the-age-of-sexual-consent.

Better Days. https://www.betterdays2020.com.

Brown, Barbara Jones. "Susan B. Anthony and Her Strong Ties with Utah." Better Days. https://www.utahwomenshistory.org/2017/12/susan-b-anthony-and-her-strong-utah-ties/

Brown, Barbara Jones, Naomi Watkins and Katherine Kitterman. "Gaining, Losing, and Winning Back the Vote: The Story of Utah Woman's Suffrage." Better Days. https://www.utahwomenshistory.org/2018/02/receiving-losing-and-winning-back-the-vote-the-story-of-utah-womens-suffrage/.

Bull, Emma. "Quilt, 1893." https://collections.lib.utah.edu/ark:/87278/s6v43p8n/128536.

Church of Jesus Christ of Latter-Day Saints. "Facts and Statistics." 2021. https://news-ie.churchofjesuschrist.org/facts-and-statistics/country/united-kingdom.

Coates, Ta-Nehisi. "The Great Schism." *Atlantic*, October 18, 2011. https://www.theatlantic.com/national/archive/2011/10/the-great-schism/246640/.

Dukakis, Andrea. "Child Marriage, Common in the Past, Persists Today." Colorado Public Radio. Aired April 4, 2017. https://www.cpr.org/show-segment/child-marriage-common-in-the-past-persists-today/.

Family Search (LDS Church's acclaimed genealogical database). https://www.familysearch.org.

Feldman, Ellen. "Till Divorce Do Us Part." *American Heritage*, November 2000. https://www.americanheritage.com/till-divorce-do-us-part.

Flores, Devin. "Which State Had Women's Suffrage First?" *History Colorado*, July 25, 2019. https://www.historycolorado.org/story/womens-history/2019/07/25/which-state-had-womens-suffrage-first.

Gopnik, Adam. "American Studies." *New Yorker*, September 20, 1998. https://www.newyorker.com/magazine/1998/09/28/american-studies.

History. "The Great Awakening." September 20, 2019. https://www.history.com/topics/british-history/great-awakening.

Jabour, Anya. "Women's Work and Sex Work in 19th Century America." PBS. February 22, 2016. https://www.pbs.org/mercy-street/blogs/mercy-street-revealed/womens-work-and-sex-work-in-nineteenth-century-america/.

Jacobs, Becky. "LDS Church Announces It Still Opposes Equal Rights Amendment as Supporters Rally at Capitol." *Salt Lake City Tribune*, December 3, 2019. https://www.sltrib.com/news/2019/12/03/lds-church-announces-it/.

Karlamangla, Soumya. "Male Doctors Are Disappearing from Gynecology. Not Everybody Is Thrilled About It." *Los Angeles Times*, March 7, 2018.

Kitterman, Katherine. "Rival Suffrage Organizations: Utah's Place in the National Movement." Better Days. https://www.utahwomenshistory.org/2019/12/rival-suffrage-organizations-utahs-place-in-the-national-movement-part-1/.

———. "Utah Women Had the Right to Vote Long Before Others—Then Had It Taken Away." *Washington Post*, February 14, 2020. https://www.washingtonpost.com/outlook/2020/02/14/utah-women-had-right-vote-long-before-others-and-then-had-it-taken-away/.

Kitterman, Katherine, and Rebekah Clark. "How Utah Women Gained the Right to Vote in 1870." Better Days. https://www.utahwomenshistory.org/2020/02/how-utah-women-gained-the-right-to-vote-in-1870-part-1/.

Loftus, Donna. "The Rise of the Victorian Middle Class." BBC. February 17, 2011. https://www.bbc.co.uk/history/british/victorians/middle_classes_01.shtml.

Lythgoe, Dennis. "Utah's Rogue Judge." *Deseret News*, February 19, 1999. https://www.deseret.com/1999/2/19/19429756/utah-s-rogue-judge-br-infamous-official-coming-back-to-life-in-family-history.

Mazziotta, Julie. "Salt Lake City Named Healthiest City in the U.S." *People*, January 5, 2018. https://people.com/health/healthiest-city-us-salt-lake-city/.

Meehan, Patrick. "Life and Death of Chicago's Great Ferris Wheel of 1893." Hyde Park Historical Society. 1964. https://hydeparkhistory.org/2015/04/27/ferris-wheel-in-the-1893-chicago-worlds-fair/.

Mulder, William. "The Peoples of Utah, Scandinavian Saga." Utah Department of Cultural and Community Engagement. 1976. https://historytogo.utah.gov/scandinavian-saga/.

Murden, Alistair, and David Kipper. "Amelia Dyer: Britain's Baby Butcher." *Medical Murders*. Spotify podcast. Aired November 4, 2020. https://www.spotify.com/us/.

National Museum of Wales. "Children in Mines." https://museum.wales/articles/1013/Children-in-Mines/.

NOAA. "A Brief History of Pollution." https://oceanservice.noaa.gov/education/tutorial_pollution/02history.html.

Olgin, Alex. "Male OB-GYNs Are Rare, but Is That a Problem?" *Morning Edition*, April 12, 2018. NPR https://www.npr.org/sections/health-shots/2018/04/12/596396698/male-ob-gyns-are-rare-but-is-that-a-problem.

Oneida Community. "Virtual Tours." https://www.oneidacommunity.org/videos.

Pinnacle Health Group. "Physician Statistics Summary." http://www.phg.com/2000/01/physician-statistics-summary/.

Reeves, Richard V., Isabel V. Sawhill and Eleanor Krause. "The Most Educated Women Are the Most Likely to Be Married." Brookings. August 19, 2016. https://www.brookings.edu/blog/social-mobility-memos/2016/08/19/the-most-educated-women-are-the-most-likely-to-be-married/.

Royal Oak Foundation. "5 (More) Things You Won't See Downton Abbey's Servants Doing." October 30, 2015. https://www.royal-oak.org/2015/10/30/5-more-things-you-wont-see-downton-abbeys-servants-doing/.

Searing, Linda. "The Big Number: Women Now Outnumber Men in Medical Schools." *Washington Post*, December 23, 2019. https://www.washingtonpost.com/health/the-big-number-women-now-outnumber-men-in-medical-schools/2019/12/20/8b9eddea-2277-11ea-bed5-880264cc91a9_story.html.

Serratore, Angela. "President Cleveland's Problem Child." *Smithsonian Magazine*, September 26, 2013. https://www.smithsonianmag.com/history/president-clevelands-problem-child-100800/.

Shaplen, Robert. "The Beecher-Tilton Affair." *New Yorker*, June 4, 1954. https://www.newyorker.com/magazine/1954/06/12/the-beecher-tilton-case-ii.

U.S. Bureau of Labor Statistics. "Marriage and Divorce: Patterns by Gender, Race, and Educational Attainment." October 2013. https://www.bls.gov/opub/mlr/2013/article/marriage-and-divorce-patterns-by-gender-race-and-educational-attainment.htm.

U.S. Census Bureau. "1880 Census: Volume 1. Statistics of the Population of the United States." https://www.census.gov/library/publications/1883/dec/vol-01-population.html.

Vassar, Lyndra. "How Medical Specialties Vary by Gender." American Medical Association. February 18, 2015. https://www.ama-assn.org/residents-students/specialty-profiles/how-medical-specialties-vary-gender.

ABOUT THE AUTHOR

J oan Jacobson is the author *Colorado Phantasmagorias: A Mashup of Biography, Fantasy, and Travel Guide*, the winner of the Colorado Authors League 2022 History Book of the Year, and the novel *Small Secrets: A Tale of Sex, Shame and Babies in Midcentury America*.

Visit us at
www.historypress.com